STRAWBALE
HOME PLANS

STRAWBALE
HOME PLANS

WAYNE J. BINGHAM AND COLLEEN F. SMITH

Gibbs Smith, Publisher

TO ENRICH AND INSPIRE HUMANKIND

Salt Lake City | Charleston | Santa Fe | Santa Barbara

To Michelle, David, Christopher, Jon, Mary, and Michael—in gratitude for your lives.

First Edition
11 10 09 08 07   5 4 3 2 1

Published by
Gibbs Smith, Publisher
PO Box 667
Layton, Utah 84041

Orders: 1.800.835.4993
www.gibbs-smith.com

Designed by Johnson Design, Inc.
Produced by TTA Design
Printed and bound in Hong Kong

Library of Congress Cataloging-in-Publication Data

Bingham, Wayne J.
  Strawbale home plans / Wayne J. Bingham, Colleen F. Smith.—1st ed.
    p. cm.
  ISBN-13: 978-1-58685-861-2
  ISBN-10: 1-58685-861-0
  1. Straw bale houses—Designs and plans. 2. Straw bale houses—
Pictorial works. I. Smith, Colleen F. II. Title. III. Title: Straw bale home plans.

TH4818.S77B56 2007
690'.837--dc22
                                        2006024564

Contents

Acknowledgments

We would like to thank the homeowners, who not only allowed us to come into their homes to photograph but who also made us feel welcome and so willingly provided us with floor plans and data and shared their stories with us. We are also greatly indebted to Mark Georgetti of Palo Santo Design in New Mexico; Kari Bremmer and Werner Heiber in Colorado; Joyce Coppinger, editor of *The Last Straw*, in Nebraska; Brad Young in Iowa; and so many others who so generously gave of their time in making arrangements and taking us to many of the homes.

We are grateful to the Colorado Straw Bale Association for their efforts in promoting strawbale building and their home tour in conjunction with their 2005 conference in Carbondale, which gave us the opportunity to visit many, though not all, of the strawbale homes in that mecca of strawbale building, and to the Green Builders Web site and their International Strawbale Registry at www.greenbuilders.com. We encourage all strawbale owners to register their buildings with them to keep their database up to date.

We would also like to commend and thank the many craftspeople who have been involved in strawbale building. We appreciate their generosity in taking time from their busy schedules to share their excitement for their work with us. There is a great community feeling engendered through natural building and working with homeowners who recognize the importance of building with concern for the environment and respect for our natural resources in mind.

We appreciate the invitation and encouragement from the people at Gibbs Smith, Publisher—especially CEO Christopher Robbins, editorial director Suzanne Taylor, and editor Aimee Stoddard—to work with them in preparing and producing this book.

We met and photographed this farmer hauling strawbales on the island of Santorini, Greece, in 1999. The image captured our imagination and served as the expression of building with strawbales: the basic building component, subject to the will of the person with the vision and the ambition to construct his or her own shelter. This book celebrates diversity in showing how vision and ambition can be manifest.

Introduction

Since the mid-1990s when the strawbale-building renaissance began, there has been a maturing body of work available to include in a book that could stimulate ideas and provide plans, photographs, and information for those wanting to design their own strawbale home.

We worked with Christopher Robbins at Gibbs Smith, Publisher, to define a broad range of building types, from small retreats and rural off-grid homes to urban houses, to explore and present along with floor plans and owner's personal experiences.

Even though you will find that we have categorized the buildings we've included in this book, we found that each building was an experiment of one. Each owner researched the available books, magazines, and periodicals, defined their needs, and then worked through a design process and construction process. What you will find here are the results of thirty-one individual, unique efforts.

We felt that you should have the story of each project by the owners and builders in their own words in addition to descriptive data, photographs, and floor plans. It seems impossible to separate the building from those who envisioned and then built it. Close reading will reveal homeowners' satisfactions, lessons learned, and recommendations. We have also added our comments at the end of each project.

Did we find trends? We did not find developers building strawbale houses speculatively on quarter-acre lots. We found individuals with different influences and constraints building in ways unique to them and their perceptions. Some used old barn timber frame structures to wrap with strawbales. Some experimented with a small studio expressing the flexible and artistic qualities of earthen plasters. Another encountered a sloping site and built with single levels on one side of the slope and multiple levels on the lower level. An Ecological Villa was built on the island of Rhodes in Greece.

We found many unique approaches to strawbale design and building based on people's needs and desires. A family of four, in which the wife and mother is confined to a wheelchair due to a climbing accident, built their single-level house with complete accessibility, from a wheel-in shower to level planning, to counters designed to allow full participation of an energetic individual. Additions were built onto older wooden structures. We discovered a delightful small guesthouse that brings to mind a French farmhouse that has a living roof. A small family on a modest budget built a cozy, intimate, lovingly plastered home in Nebraska.

Curves were used creatively. Susie Harrington and Kalen Jones explored the articulation of walls and roofs in several of their passive solar designs. Many other owners and builders used the inherent moldability of plastered strawbale construction to bring curvilinear walls into their environment.

Are there areas of the country where strawbale seems to flourish? Yes. One pioneer builds and sets an example; others then follow. Fairfield, Iowa, has a number of structures influenced by the Sthapatya Veda principles. Carbondale, Colorado, was the site of a strawbale home tour with sixteen different structures within a twenty-mile radius. Teton Valley, Idaho, has two dozen. Moab, Utah, has structures numbering in the twenties.

We found many more projects than could be included here. We are aware of strawbale building in China, Japan, Australia, Saudi Arabia, and many countries in Europe.

There are numerous architects, designers, and craftspeople developing skills needed to design, construct, and finish strawbale buildings, exploring the potential of earthen, lime, and other plasters. The services of these professionals are becoming available to future strawbale builders to help achieve their dreams.

Our previous strawbale learning experience was with small, owner-built structures. We again found many of these wonderful structures during our research for this book, but we also discovered a wide variety of other approaches in our travels. We encountered larger community buildings, including a dojo, a bird sanctuary, and a school. They are included to illustrate the diversity of expression available to this humble yet versatile material.

—Wayne and Colleen

SINGLE-LEVEL COUNTRY HOMES

360-Degree Views
Around Cedar Jack Mesa

Schneider Residence • Moab, Utah

Our Story

"The decision to build a strawbale home was easy. We like the natural-feeling energy that straw provides compared to steel and concrete. After sleeping for many years on a straw mattress in a bed built strictly with wood, we were not prepared to compromise building our dream house.

"As in any project, people were also key to the success of our project. We wanted views to all four directions in the kitchen and living room, and a courtyard in the east to provide shelter from the heat in summer. Local natural-building designer Susie Harrington put all our ideas into an executable layout and building plan, which met county regulations.

"While Susie added her signature barrel-top roof to the design and fine tuned the construction plan, we entered all our furniture measurements into a computer program. This allowed us to view our future house in 3-D with all furniture in place and make adjustments to windows, doors, and walls in the layout so everything would fit into the new house.

"Our builder, Jeff Johnston, had long-time construction experience and the ability to assemble a fantastic crew and subcontractors. His ingenuity along with the German engineering from our friend, Joachim Maehner, proved to be invaluable in solving every tricky issue in the realization of our creative ideas.

"Jeff's initial cost estimate for materials was right on. Labor proved to be less predictable because of our use of natural and indigenous materials for an environmentally friendly building. We used strawbales from Colorado, geothermal heating and cooling, pumice for the floor insulation, prickly pear cactus juice as glue in adobe mud floors, clay from the Colorado River, natural rocks from the surrounding canyons, fire-kill juniper logs from the mountains, and car tires from the landfill for the retaining wall.

"We located the strawbales through Fry Brothers Farmers a year ahead to adjust the wall height to the strawbale size. Larry Kleine, an experienced strawbale consultant from Phoenix, Arizona, trained our crew and us in the unique way of building with straw.

"Donald Kiffmeyer and Kaki Hunter shared with us their vast knowledge of earth plaster for all walls, inside and outside. *Theory of Colours* by Johann Wolfgang von Goethe along with Donald Kaufman and Taffy Dahl's book *Color* gave us our foundation for selecting the inside colors, which were actually mixed into the plaster.

The living room wing viewed from the west at sunset has windows on three sides. A curved wraparound porch is supported by native juniper poles, which sit on a stone foundation that melds into Cedar Jack Mesa.

Specifications	
Exterior Area:	2,940 Square Feet
Interior Area:	2,400 Square Feet
Designer/Architect:	Susie Harrington and Kalen Jones
Contractor/Builder:	Jeff Johnston, Joachim Maehner
Structural System:	Post and Beam with Strawbale Infill
Exterior Plaster:	Cement Stucco
Interior Plaster:	Earthen
Bales:	Wheat Bales Laid Flat

Lessons learned:

- "A house in the desert needs rain gutters. It was a bad decision on our part to not add them against better advice. We had to add rain gutters the next year.
- "Not all earth is created equal. The earth on our land proved too smooth for wall plaster, so we had to add sharp-edged quartz sand. The plaster on our test wall was great, but the same plaster on the real wall did not work as expected.
- "Our geothermal system is laid horizontally in the ground. Laying the system vertically would have been more efficient, but initial cost is a factor to consider.
- "Retaining walls built from used tires look good in books but require hard, long work and lots of sand. The advantage, besides recycling, is that we could easily adjust the walls later in the process.
- "Pumice comes in powder and in inch-sized pebbles. Clarify which you will be buying before ordering; otherwise you might be surprised, as we were.
- "If the staff in the local branch of your bank is supportive and helpful but the underwriters in the bank headquarters are not, it might be worthwhile to consider using a local mortgage broker, even if the cost is higher."

—Kira and Eric

Kira.

Natural light floods the terra-cotta, earthen-plastered walls and the oiled earthen floor of the hall leading from the guest room to the main entry.

Single-Level Country Homes

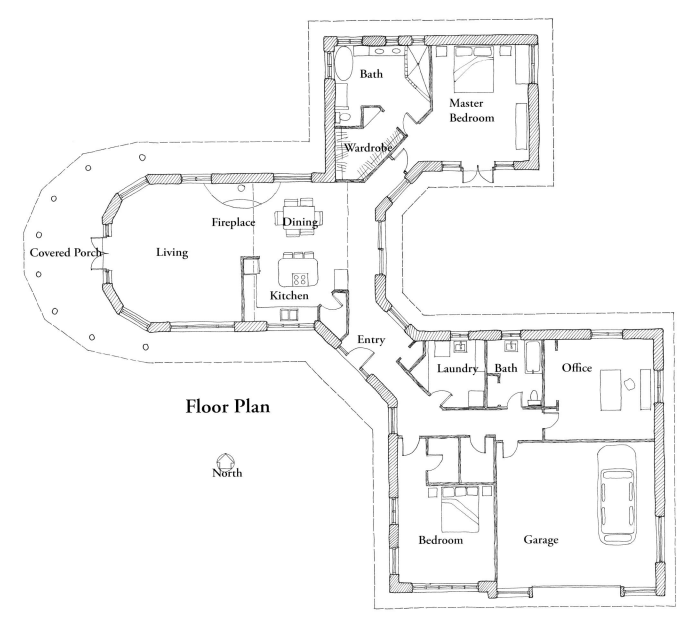

Floor Plan

North

Colorful, Calm, and Serene

This beautiful home on Cedar Jack Mesa takes advantage of the surrounding 360-degree dynamic views with changing clouds and light. There are three distinct zones; the garage/guest/study/mechanical wing, the living/kitchen/dining wing, and the master bedroom suite. The designers chose to offset each wing from the others so each space would have access to direct natural light and air. Most living spaces have light on at least two sides of every room, balancing the light and reducing the potential glare from one side. Circulation is clear and hallways are minimized.

Light-filled and colorful, the ambiance changes with the movement of the sun through the sky during the day. Earthen floors throughout combine with the natural-colored walls and ceiling to produce a calming and serene effect.

A curved kiva fireplace is visible from both the living room and kitchen/dining room. The curved, stepped-down partition between the living room and kitchen is terminated by a juniper pole.

Single-Level Country Homes

The soft plaster colors of the master bathroom glow in the late-afternoon light. The tub is surrounded with native stone. The glass block–enclosed walk-in shower is to the right. Kira designed and laid the river stone patterns in the floor.

Single-Level Country Homes

The kitchen is situated as the central hub for the wings of the home with a clerestory window and vaulted ceiling. The built-in island houses the sink, and the counter extends for bar stools. The living room wing is to the right. A pantry is enclosed with curved-top terra-cotta walls to the left.

The south face of the home takes advantage of solar access by use of large windows into the living room area, which look out to the pinion and juniper desert forest. The stone foundation is carried up to the window sill of the bedroom wing, with coral-colored, lime-plastered walls above.

Structure Harmonizing with a Treed Mesa Setting

Drinker-Durrance Residence • Carbondale, Colorado

Our Story

"When we were younger, we seriously considered building a log cabin home. This fantasy lasted exactly the amount of time it took us to set up a meeting with a reputable architect. As numbers beat down upon us, we acknowledged that we could, indeed, have our dream home, as long as we were okay with a quarter acre in the outermost reaches of eastern Mongolia.

"Many years passed as we struggled to find our place in successive locations progressively farther down the Roaring Fork Valley, usually sacrificing something in the hopes that the total package was worth more than the sum of its parts. It just never quite fit.

"Then, one night at a birthday party, a friend began speaking of building with bales. The idea captivated me, and after a few days online and a meeting with a local straw man of national repute, the idea became firmly entrenched in both my husband's and my sensibilities, and the process began. As with any birth, the best-laid plans fall asunder.

"As luck would have it, tiny Carbondale, Colorado, is one of the epicenters of bale technology, and Keith Brand, a local builder, was a goldmine of ideas and expertise . . . with one major drawback. He and Jeff Dickinson, the green-sustainable architect he builds with, were about to embark on a one-year sailing sabbatical. As Dad used to say, 'Damn the torpedoes! Full speed ahead.' Keith turned us on to our builder, John

Stewart, and Jeff initiated the planning process and passed us on to Donna Riley, our architect, and therein you have the whole fiber of baling—teamwork and community.

"It couldn't have happened any other way. John was unfazed by a building without the exterior 'sticks' he was used to, and Donna embraced each innovative idea with grace and cunning. That's the thing with strawbale; it is so innovative you just cannot be too far out in the scope of your dreams, and budget for that matter.

"If I hadn't succumbed to a few exotic embellishments, $150 per square foot would not have been hard to adhere to. We set our sights on the loveliest two acres of ancient pinion forest in the valley.

"My most humble gratitude and appreciation goes to the architectural review committee at Elk Springs for their progressive thinking and positive attitude. Their suggestions in the interest of the community codes actually brought our home to a higher level of aesthetic sensibility than we probably could have achieved on our own. On the exterior, our home is virtually indistinguishable from the forest it shares and totally in conformance with the upscale neighborhood.

"Next, the fear factor . . . we were the first bale structure to use lime plaster instead of concrete. Lime plaster is organic, but a bunch of oysters is the only thing between you and the alpine elements. Yes,

Specifications	
Exterior Area:	2,160 Square Feet
Interior Area:	1,750 Square Feet
Designer/Architect:	Donna L. Riley and Jeff Dickinson
Contractor/Builder	John B. Stewart
Structural System:	Modified Post and Beam with Strawbale Infill
Exterior Plaster:	Lime over Metal Lath with Integral Color for Final Coat
Interior Plaster:	Lime over Metal Lath with Integral Color for Final Coat
Bales:	Two-String Wheat Laid Flat with Rebar Pinning

and a healthier long-term life to boot. Again, the aid of experts from around the country wading in with suggestions and support, and 1,200 tons of French lime plaster has set us in a class by ourselves.

"The ancient trees we had to displace are now supporting the porch and patio deck, and the heat-recovery system provides fresh air without the heating bills. The interior colors are vibrant and sensual, the carefully carved niches frame our favorite possessions, and our cat has a million deep window vantage points for monitoring the daily parade of turkeys and other wildlife. We are home."

—Sue and Dick

A view from the kitchen toward the living area with an exposed-beam vaulted ceiling. The dining area is to the left. Just beyond the volcanic stone fountain is the entrance to Sue's photographic studio. Natural light from the south-facing windows floods the living room. The elliptical arch that encloses the bookshelves and art wall anchors the room.

Single-Level Country Homes

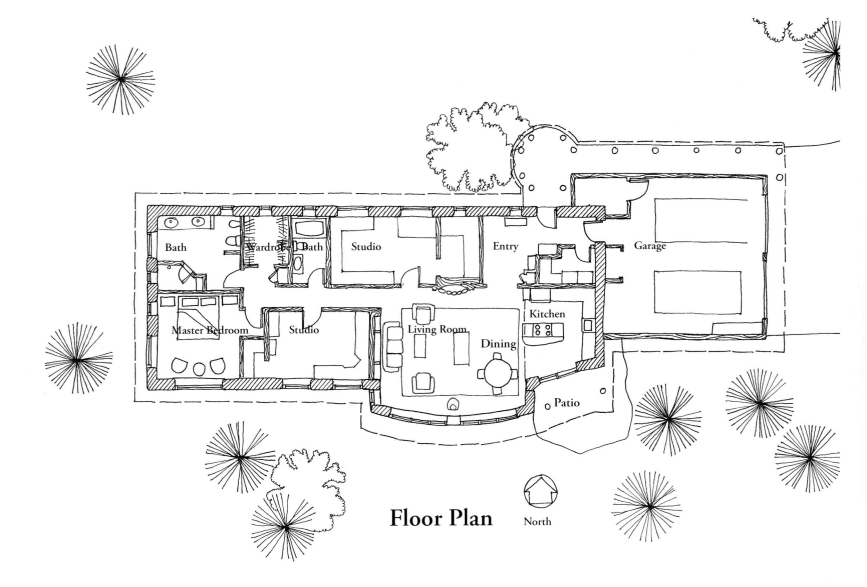

Floor Plan

North

Ancient Pinion Forest Setting

Situated on a tree-covered mesa above Carbondale, this house blends the use of stone, plaster, and red-framed windows with the stone and pinion pine trees surrounding the house. Care was taken to only minimally disturb the vegetation during construction.

The entry on the north leads through a graceful elliptical arch to the living/dining spaces with a beamed cathedral ceiling. High windows admit ample south light. We found the living/dining space with the arched bookshelves and art alcove at the west end to be almost magical. Our eyes and camera lenses kept going back there. The kitchen is

adjacent to the living/dining space under a lower ceiling, almost an alcove off the larger space. The plan is articulated to allow a small outdoor dining area just outside the kitchen.

Two home offices are immediately off the living area. The master bedroom is at the extreme west end of the house. These rooms have light on two sides of the space, making each bright and airy. The color scheme is soft and restful with butter yellow in the main living areas, a muted blue in the bedroom, and a sage green in the bathroom. Persian rugs adorn the stained concrete floors in the living areas.

A view from the living area toward the left entrance. The entrance vestibule is large enough to provide a gracious welcome to guests. The kitchen is in the center and dining is to the right. The kitchen has light on two sides and a lowered ceiling.

Single-Level Country Homes

The top of the blue-painted walls of the bedroom slopes to a darker blue ceiling. Nature is brought into the room with a vine-covered trellis on one wall.

Natural light brightens the soft green bathroom. There are individual sinks, mirrors, and lights. The shower is to the left.

13

The stark desert setting contrasts with the rectangular shapes of the house.

Accessible Desert Home

Horning-Riedel Residence • Big Water, Utah

Our Story

"Eight years before building a home, my husband, Pat, was set on constructing a cinder block structure. As I described energy-efficient alternatives and brought home the book *The Straw Bale House*, he became fascinated with this technique. Our first step was to purchase, instead of a new car, a beautiful three-acre property in southern Utah, bordered by Grand Staircase National Monument, Lake Powell, and Vermillion Cliffs National Monument. We acquired the land through owner financing, and after paying this loan off over five years we began searching for an architect and a mortgage lender.

"We found Pam Wells who was very excited to have the opportunity to be involved in a strawbale home. Based on our extremely detailed floor plan, she created complete architectural drawings for a load-bearing home. For three years, we were told by an agent of a local lending company that our home would be financially possible. One month before construction was to begin the agent told us that our interest rate for our nontraditional home would be twice as much as for a traditional home—thus financially eliminating our dream. However, we literally walked across the street to a young new financer who had his own lending company, and before the day's end, he had our project financed at the regular rates of October 2000. We also were able to receive a break on our homeowner's insurance due to the positive fire-resistant aspects of strawbale construction.

"Pat has many construction skills and I have endless creative ideas, but neither of us had built an entire home and our financing required a licensed contractor. We found a local contractor willing to allow us to cut costs by completing any projects that we could through sweat equity. By building our home in this way, we were able to construct our 4,000-square-foot home for $45 per square foot.

"Here is a simplified outline of the work done by the contractor or by us:

"May 2000: We obtained complete architectural drawings, received approval from the local building inspector to build a strawbale home, and located a licensed contractor willing to allow us to include our own sweat equity.

"October 2000: We acquired traditional financing with our property used as the down payment.

"November 2000: The contractor and subs dug and prepared the site with my diligent direction to do as little damage as possible to the native vegetation. We set the foam insulation and tied rebar and the tubing for a radiant floor. The contractor and subs poured the foundation at the end of the month.

Specifications	
Exterior Area:	4,000 Square Feet
Interior Area:	3,270 Square Feet
Designer/Architect:	Pam Wells
Contractor/Builder:	Ark Builders and Owners
Structural System:	Load-Bearing Strawbales
Exterior Plaster:	Cement Plaster Applied Pneumatically and with Trowels
Interior Plaster:	Gypsum Applied by Hand
Bales:	Three-String Barley Laid Flat and Pre-compressed, Rebar Internal Pinning

The living room, with its Southwest-style fireplace and outdoor patio beyond.

The dining room and kitchen within the lofty great room are filled with natural light from two sides. The Southwest-style post and beams with corbels define the kitchen cabinet space and the entry to the bedroom and garage. The freestanding island includes a cooktop and sink for easy wheelchair access.

Porch with view of the desert in the afternoon rain.

"January 2001: After letting the foundation cure for a month, we gathered a group of twenty-five friends and family to stack the bales. We were expecting this to take a week, but it actually only took one and a half days. At completion, all window and door bucks were set. Two family members helped the contractor set the top plate and roof trusses.

"Pat spent ten days trimming and straightening the bale walls with a chain saw, preparing them for stucco. We should have spent a little more time straightening the bales as we stacked them and eliminating the time to even the bales afterwards. With the contractor, we positioned a system of banding to compact the walls as the bales settled. We adjusted this banding over the next two weeks.

"February–March 2001: The extensive porches and only supporting wall in our home were built by the contractor using recycled telephone poles. Electrical lines and outlets were set into the straw walls by an electrician. We helped set the 2 x 4 framing for the interior room divisions. The plumber set the plumbing lines necessary before gypsum board work began.

"April–August 2001: A roofing contractor installed a latex fifty-year roof. We helped apply metal roofs to the porches. The contractor built low cinder block division walls in the bathrooms, bedroom, and living room, and we applied native stone surfaces.

"We prepared the interior and exterior walls for cement stucco with two weeks of pinning, tar paper, and chicken wire. Originally, we had hired a local couple to hand stucco our walls inside and out. However, after seeing the time-consuming work of plastering stucco by hand on uneven bale walls, our contractor hired a crew to apply by machine the first two coats of cement stucco. Then the exterior and interior of the walls were finished by hand.

"Over the next couple of months, we did a lot of site cleanup. We painted all interior walls, doors, and trim. We stained and finished the concrete floors. We helped the contractor build concrete countertops in the kitchen and bathroom. We etched designs into windows. We shopped for lighting and cabinetry fixtures, appliances, and doors and drove them to the site, a very time-consuming project.

"The contractor and subs set a septic system. The plumber finished setting the fixtures. The electrician set the lighting, switches, and electrical boxes. A local cabinetmaker built and aligned the cabinets to fit the uneven straw walls. A tile setter tiled our master bathroom shower. After the double-paned sliding windows were set in place, we noticed some problems with the bracing above two windows set in load-bearing walls. We had to reconstruct the bracing for these two windows, our only difficulty with the home's construction process.

"September 2001: After a final inspection by the city building inspector, our construction loan was rolled over into permanent financing as we had planned, and we moved into our beautiful home.

"Although we have the system for a solar water heated floor, we have yet to set the solar panels and solar tank. Our home has a heat pump and a propane fireplace. After five years of living in the home, the energy efficiency of the straw walls is evident by our low heating bills; we rarely use the heating-and-cooling system. Our home seems to stay an even, comfortable temperature most days of the year even with 100-plus degrees Fahrenheit in the summer and nights at 20 degrees Fahrenheit in the winter. We use the propane fireplace for a couple of evening hours in the winter.

"All visitors who spend time at our home comment on the beauty and comfort. With the exception of modern amenities, the structure feels like a two-hundred-year-old thick-walled Spanish mission."

—Lisa and Pat

Stone tile covers the walls and floor of the shower. The glass block admits natural light while obscuring the view into the shower. The space between the exterior wall and the glass-block wall is wide enough to allow full wheelchair access to the shower.

A built-in bed, with plaster headboard, niches, and shelves, provides space for art. The deep red wall contrasts with the natural headboard.

Desert Home Near Lake Powell

We were very impressed with how this house is graciously designed to allow full mobility for Lisa, who was injured in a hiking accident and is now in a wheelchair. When we arrived, she was out on her ride, keeping fit in her cycle.

The home has three living zones: master bedroom and bathing area with garage space to the north; great room with kitchen, dining room, and living room in the center; and a children's bedroom/bathroom zone to the south. A covered porch to the east provides weather protection for the entrance that leads into the great room.

The master bathing area is unique with a curved glass-block wall spaced to allow wheelchair access directly into the shower. A sink is at a convenient height with sufficient room behind for wheelchair access. The master bed is built in with plastered adobe headboard with lights and places for books and art. A deep red wall behind the bed accents the headboard.

Covered outdoor patios off the master bedroom and the great room provide exterior living spaces when weather permits.

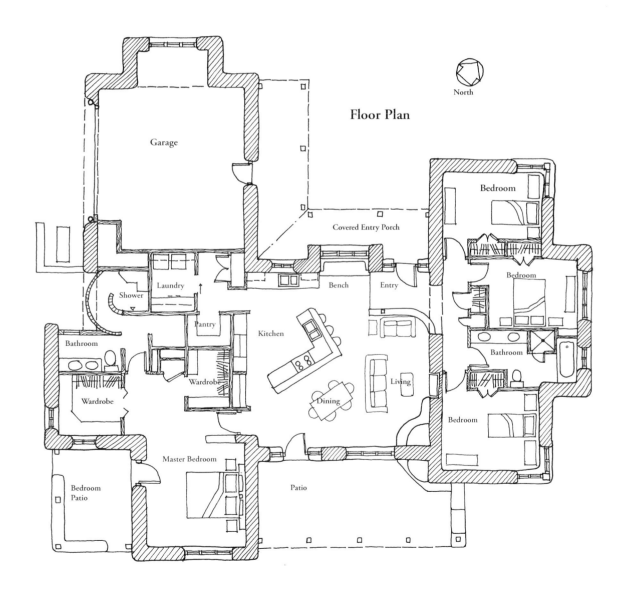

North

Floor Plan

Garage

Covered Entry Porch

Laundry

Shower

Bench

Entry

Pantry

Kitchen

Bathroom

Wardrobe

Living

Bathroom

Wardrobe

Dining

Bedroom

Master Bedroom

Patio

Bedroom
Patio

The contrasting colors and distinct shapes of this home differentiate building elements.
The extended overhang protects the south face from the sun.

Two Simple Forms
Connected by a Soft Link

Huttenhower Residence • Carbondale, Colorado

Our Story

"Rich and I found a great piece of land in the middle of an old hayfield near Carbondale with a spectacular view of Mt. Sopris, a 12,900-foot mountain. The setting inspired us to build something beautiful and natural and after mulling over some log plans that our subdivision rejected, we decided to investigate strawbale. There are a few very beautiful straw homes close by that we visited and that led to our final decision to seek out strawbale builders Mark Wolfe of Wolfe-Brand Construction and the Jacober Brothers of JBC Construction. They collaborated on the project with my husband, who served as general contractor, and our architect Michael Hassig of A4 architects, whom we knew and respected both personally and professionally.

"After six months of planning, we broke ground in the spring and moved in that December just in time for an onslaught of holiday guests. The process was educational for everyone, especially those of us who were involved in strawbale construction for the first time. We definitely made some miscalculations on things like window placements, light switches, and drainage for the washer and the ventilation for the dryer. We also poured our back slab too soon, we had concrete stain leech up our already stuccoed walls, and we had some general miscommunication with subcontractors.

"But perhaps the most interesting error of judgment was in how we chose to protect our straw pile. Fearful of spring rain, we tightly covered our straw stash with tarp and rope, only later to discover that we had actually caused more damage by doing so. The water that got in could not escape, and we had to replace many rotting bales. This was a great lesson in strawbale construction as well as life. It became so clear why you should not try to overprotect anything. You may wind up suffocating it. A house needs to breathe, especially a strawbale house.

"I think the combination of smallness, openness, flow, simplicity, natural materials, and traditional lines distinguishes our home. It's a nice blend of old and new, and the space is beautiful and utilitarian. Building our home has meant a lot to us, and we feel fortunate to have been involved in the process of creating something so personal and then sharing that creation with a growing family, friends, and visitors from abroad who come to retreat in our home."

—Rich and Ellen

Specifications	
Exterior Area:	1,870 Square Feet
Interior Area:	1,528 Square Feet
Designer/Architect:	Michael Hassig
Contractor/Builder:	Owner-Builder
Structural System:	Hybrid Post and Beam
Exterior Plaster:	Cement Stucco on Metal Lath with Gypsum Topcoat
Interior Plaster:	Cement Stucco on Metal Lath with Gypsum Topcoat
Bales:	Two-String Wheat Straw with Bamboo Pinning

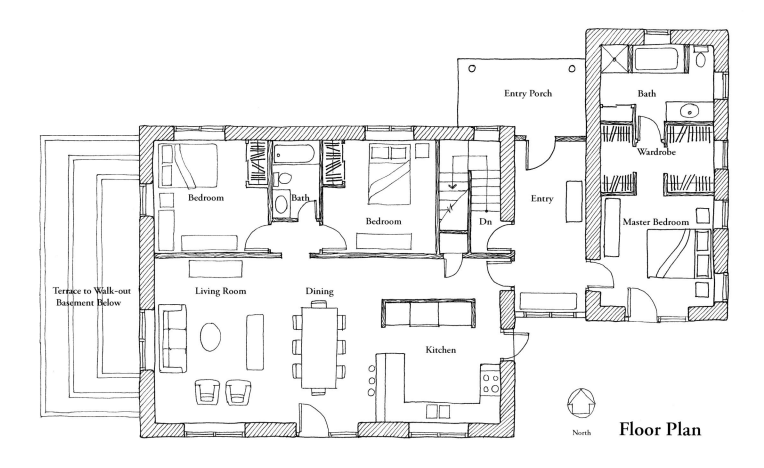

Terrace to Walk-out
Basement Below

Bedroom

Bath

Living Room

Dining

Kitchen

Bedroom

Dn

Entry

Entry Porch

Bath

Wardrobe

Master Bedroom

North

Floor Plan

Separate Family
Living and Master Suite

Two simple shapes connected by a "soft link" entrance are an elegant solution to this unique plan.

The east wing includes the master suite with bedroom, bath, and walk-in closet. There is a ship's ladder leading up to a loft above the wardrobe and bathroom, while the master bed enjoys the one-and-a-half-story cathedral ceiling.

The west wing includes two bedrooms, kitchen, and living and dining spaces. The bedrooms are in a lower ceiling shed-roofed portion off the living area. The kitchen and living and dining areas share a single space with a one-and-a-half-story wood-paneled cathedral ceiling.

There is a full basement under the west wing that has a walk-out door leading to a small patio.

A wood-covered cathedral ceiling with skylights unifies the living/dining/kitchen spaces.

Niches provide places to display objects, such as flowers, candles, and art.

24

The rounded, deep windows
and door jambs capture and
reflect light into the lofty
master bedroom suite.

The moon rises over the mountain at sunset, with house and garage nestled into the native vegetation.

Long, Linear House
with a Lap Pool

Simone-Crutchfield Residence • Moab, Utah

Our Story

"Our motivation to build our home with strawbale grew out of our desire to build 'easy on the earth.' We contacted the American Institute of Architects to help us connect with Kenton Peters II, an architect who cares about the environment, and it was he who educated us about options. We visited a strawbale home and were drawn to its cocoon-like feel.

"Three months into construction, with the walls in place but not yet stuccoed, the house burned to the ground due to a spark from a grinding machine. The fire was an amazing 'purification' of intention and commitment and it further strengthened relationships with everyone on the project. Our contractor immediately reserved replacement trestle wood for our posts and beams. There was a limited supply of this one-hundred-year-old Douglas fir from the Great Salt Lake rail line, another important part of our project.

"Our home might be thought of as unique due to the 75-foot lap pool immediately inside the front door. We weren't sure that the humidity of the pool would work in conjunction with the strawbale. Jan traded a series of massage-therapy sessions with a mechanical engineer to do those calculations. The heat-exchange ventilators he recommended have done the job. The house is unique, in part, because of its Asian feel. As dedicated meditators, we are deeply grateful for the quiet of our site. The strawbale insulation and its 'softness' enhance our experiencing of our home as a refuge.

"The process of designing and building our home and recently redecorating it has been deeply instructive. The redecorating brought in cork and Marmoleum, 'Korea board' made of compressed sorghum stalks, recycled glass mixed into concrete, and 50-percent recycled tile. It has been exciting to witness the increasing availability of these more sustainable products, but it still amazes us that it is so painstaking and expensive to acquire them. Non-VOC paint was cost prohibitive when we first built as were the solar aspects of design we would have preferred.

"We feel good about the choices we were able to make that we believe support a healthier way to live. We would definitely use strawbale again, although we cannot envision the need or desire to build another home."

—Jan and Cliff

Specifications	
Exterior Area:	1,925 Square Feet
Interior Area:	1,600 Square Feet
Designer/Architect:	Kenton Peters II
Contractor/Builder:	Tom Rees
Structural System:	Post and Beam
Exterior Plaster:	Cement-Based Stucco on Chicken Wire
Interior Plaster:	Gypsum
Bales:	Wheat Straw Laid Flat

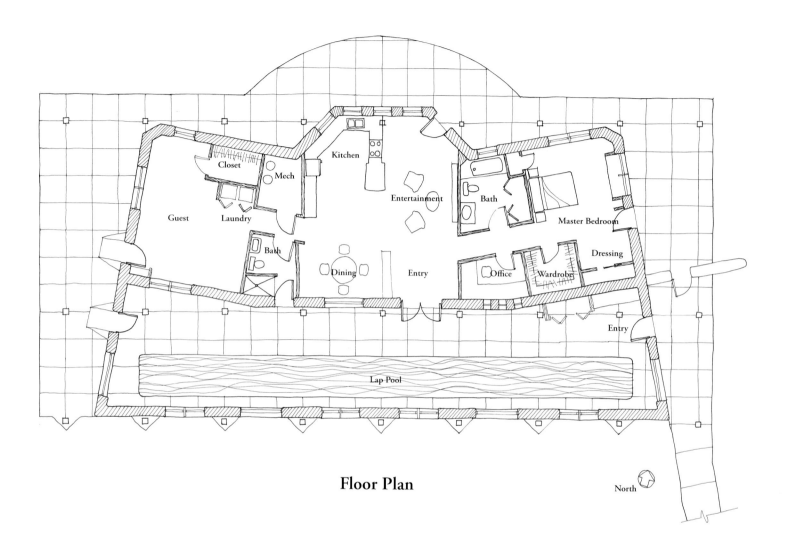

Floor Plan

North

Serenity at the Base of the Mountain

Architect Kenton Peters II nestled the long building into the natural vegetation at the base of the mountain with the long axis running east and west for solar gain to the lap pool, which runs the length of the house.

The central living, dining, and kitchen great room share a high-ceiling clerestory space with windows on the north and south and glass block on the east and west to minimize heat gain. The bedroom, wardrobe, study, and guest room occupy the lower roofed wings.

The house is in a dry desert environment and has roof extensions on the north, east, and west to shelter exterior patios from direct sun to allow west use in the morning and east in the evening. The north side is protected during the daytime hours. Soft colors and a natural cork floor create a quiet background for photographic and other artistic expression. The furniture selection and arrangement all combine to give a serene and elegant feel to the home.

The lofty, curved clerestory ceiling floats over and unifies living/kitchen/dining and house entrance areas.

The deep, east-facing entrance shows off wall thickness.

Built-in storage on the right side of the bed and windows on two sides of the room create a serene atmosphere in the master bedroom.

South-facing windows admit passive heat and light into the room containing the lap pool.

The 75-foot lap pool is flooded with natural light. Infill strawbale walls surround the lap pool room, and the roof loads are supported by an exposed post-and-beam structural system. The cast-in-place concrete lap pool is the full length of the room and provides a place for Jan and Cliff to exercise indoors.

Single-Level Country Homes

The simple shed roof is raised above the south-facing wall to admit generous passive solar heat and light.
The projecting metal-clad enclosure houses a couch and stove.

Home Displaying Creative Use of Recycled Materials

Powers-Hanson Residence • Victor, Idaho

Our Story

"We began building our house in the spring of 2004. We were fortunate to have friends and family who helped us immensely through the whole building process. Aaron's father and sister and my sister stayed with us that summer to help. We lived in a compound of two RVs, a tipi, a wall tent, and a small sauna building converted to a bathroom. Our plan was to build a small strawbale house with no construction loan. Thus, local and salvaged materials, a small footprint, and sweat equity were all really important.

"Our house is largely a mix of many past houses. It started with a trip to the dump one day that culminated in our returning with more than we left with. It was amazing the great things we found: doors, chairs, windows, lumber, drills and many more valuable materials. Throughout the building process, we frequented the dumps. Before long, word got out about our dump diving. We were made aware of a few

houses slated for the dump that had not yet been demolished. This was even better. We embarked on a two-month spree of retrieving material and objects slated for the landfill.

"One of these houses provided about 85 percent of the lumber and timber, all windows, most doors, floor tiles, appliances, and chimney pipe, as well as things such as the paint mixer, the BBQ grills, clothes (retro '70s), and an elevator that we have not used yet. Our shower/tub is made of redwood we removed from a sauna room being torn down. The bathroom tile is a past kitchen countertop tile (chipped off the counter tile by tile). And our deep windowsills are beetle-killed pine that a friend found in the dump.

"The north, east, and west walls of the house are strawbale. We chose straw because of its insulating properties and because there is so much of it here in Teton Valley. The exterior plaster is a lime mix we made on-site. And the interior plaster is earthen, consisting of local clay, sand, and straw. Our south wall is largely glass, so we framed it conventionally and used recycled denim insulation. Some materials that we couldn't find, we bought salvaged. The metal on both the roof and ceiling is reclaimed from old sheds in Montana. The roof is insulated with blown-in recycled-content cellulose.

"The footprint of our house is less than 850 square feet. With two people and two large dogs, we needed to plan some space-saving ideas

Aaron and Meghan.

Specifications	
Exterior Area:	800 Square Feet
Interior Area:	666 Square Feet
Designer/Architect:	Aaron Powers and Meghan Hanson
Contractor/Builder:	Owners and Family
Structural System:	Post and Beam
Exterior Plaster:	Earthen-and-Lime Plaster
Interior Plaster:	Earthen Plaster
Bales:	Two-String Wheat Flat with Bamboo Pinning

into the house. Thus, our dining table is sunken in the floor and there is a removable piece over it. This area transitions between being the living room and the dining room. Part of our redwood shower is a focal point in the living room. Also, there are no walls between the living room and kitchen. The enclosed areas, like closets and the bathroom, have low ceilings to allow the main ceiling to extend above and give the house an open feel.

"Building our house was an eye-opening experience for us. Our heating bill was the same in July and August as it was in December and January. We turned off our radiant heat. With the south glazing and a dark floor, the sun heats our house. When it's cloudy, a small pellet stove is plenty to warm the house. In the summer, the overhang on our roof shields the south wall from the sun, leaving it in shade for most of the day. High windows combined with windows on the north, west, and east promote cooling ventilation.

"Along with the house, we placed a 27-foot-diameter grain silo on-site. We bought it from a local farmer who no longer used it. We added two levels in it and now use it as a studio/shop above and sailboat storage below. All the lumber and plywood are reclaimed from destroyed houses. We still have our own 'lumberyard' out back.

"Our house and outbuildings are still in process, and I think they may always be. A trip to the dump is now prefaced by a little excited anticipation. What will we find today?"

—Aaron and Meghan

Mortgage Free

On property they had traded for work, Meghan and Aaron wanted to build a house with salvaged materials, personal effort, and only the money they could allocate from their income. To be mortgage free was the objective.

Many of the structural materials were salvaged from houses being remodeled in a neighboring city. The ceiling is recycled corrugated, galvanized steel. The roof projects to the north to provide covered outdoor storage. The strawbales were inexpensive as was the earthen plaster inside and out. Cabinets were made with exposed wheat board and then oiled.

The house is heated with a pellet stove located next to a built-in sofa in a bay projecting south of the living area. The dining area is in a recessed well in the earthen floor. A removable lid reveals a wood table and two opposing built-in benches below.

If one wants to live mortgage free and has a lot of ingenuity and energy, one can build his or her dream home.

As a space-saving strategy, the dining table is recessed into the floor and can be covered to become the living area. The kitchen and entrance are beyond.

The recessed dining area is in the foreground next to the kitchen on the right. On the left is the pellet stove and built-in seating. The back of the cylindrical shower projects out into the living space.

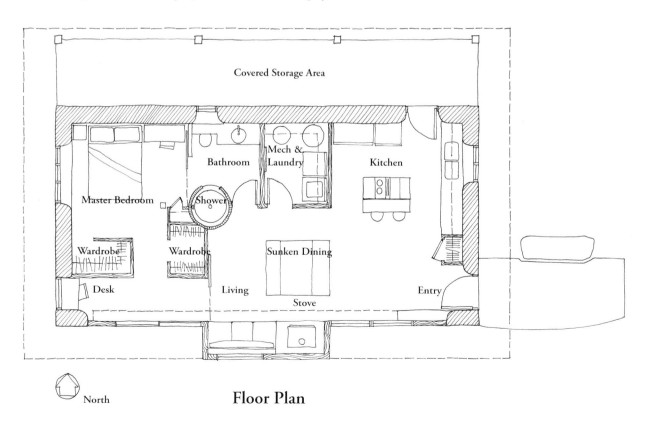

Covered Storage Area

Bathroom

Mech & Laundry

Kitchen

Master Bedroom

Shower

Wardrobe

Wardrobe

Sunken Dining

Desk

Living

Stove

Entry

North

Floor Plan

Morning light just touching the curved roof silhouetted against Castle Rock.

Passive Solar Abode
with a Softly Curved Roof

O'Brien Residence • Castle Valley, Utah

Our Story

"Building a strawbale house felt perfect: the enjoyment of passive solar warmth in the cold winter and insulated coolness in the hot summer; the use of on-site materials; the chance to join with friends to help with construction; and the ease of making everything rounded: corners, niches, arches, and walls. We were able to locate local discarded bowling alley wood for the bed, built-in benches, and outdoor dining table. We located burned juniper for posts and recycled old-growth wood for the indoor table. The dirt floor (sealed with linseed oil and a nontoxic finish) allows us to walk on our site's earth. The house faces south with an almost solid bank of windows, letting in every moment of short winter sun, while the shaded eastern patio and roof keep all direct summer sun out.

"The house was pure joy to build with local workers, most of whom live a few blocks away. The designer showed us how the roof might be curved. The framer was a former furniture maker, building the whole house like he would a comfortable rocking chair. Our electrician lives off-grid. Our strawbaler is an artist who would go into the local mountains predawn to paint before coming down to teach us how to put up the bales and slap on mud. The woman who finished the inside walls and tiling had built her own small strawbale house; she kept bringing us amenities from her home before we had this home as shelter.

"There is one thing we would do differently: the local well driller installed PVC pipe before we even thought to discuss other less-toxic piping options with him, which include PEX or copper.

"We were able to build this house in large part with money our mother-in-law/mother left when she passed away. She was not a wealthy woman but had always lived modestly in a small house herself. Our 800-square-foot house feels spacious and graciously beautiful, and it is warm in winter, cool in summer, quiet, and open to our desert world.

"And now, we are working to restore native plants to our five-acre site dominated by cheat grass. It's all part of becoming more and more seamless with the world around us."

—Mary and Bob

Mary and Bob.

Specifications	
Exterior Area:	1,070 Square Feet
Interior Area:	860 Square Feet
Designer/Architect:	Susie Harrington and Kalen Jones
Contractor/Builder:	Owner
Structural System:	Post and Beam
Exterior Plaster:	Earthen Plaster
Interior Plaster:	Earthen Plaster
Bales:	Barley Laid Flat

The southeast corner of the building with a low garden wall and canvas awning creates shaded exterior living space.

The dining space occupies a south-facing bay window with generous overhang that provides protection from the summer sun.

Single-Level Country Homes

Intriguing Curves

We saw this house under construction several years ago and were enamored with the soft, sensual curve of the roof set against the backdrop of the deep red sandstone monolith Castle Rock. We still are. The roof hovers over the house that is elongated east and west, with just enough overhang to protect the glazing from overheating the interior during the hot Castle Valley summers. We tried photographing the home during the summer, but all of our photos showed dark shadows under the roof. Yet in the winter, the sun dives deep into the house, providing welcome light and heat.

Juniper posts support a generous canvas patio shade cloth extending east and south in a broad semicircle. The deep red earthen plaster blends with the stone mountains that surround Castle Valley. Inside, the earthen floor supports the soft red earthen plastered walls and allows the reed-mat ceiling to soar overhead. The dining area is set into a bay window on the south of the living area, opposite the kitchen. Long, high windows below the curved roof bring light in and softly illuminate the ceiling.

The reed-mat ceiling arches over the dining area and continues over the low partition to the office space beyond.

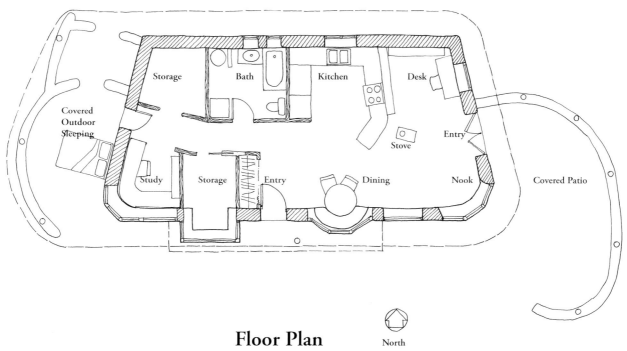

Floor Plan

North

MULTILEVEL COUNTRY HOMES

Ranch Site
Two-Story Home

Andersen-Rehorn Residence • Durango, Colorado

Our Story

"When Kathy and I were married, her grandmother bought us a table saw so that I could build our house. That was in 1989. It can be fairly said that I took my sweet time living up to the bargain that Granny's gift implied. It gets better—our house was started in May of 2001 and we didn't move into it until January 2005. What took us so long? Well, we studied building methods, roof lines, materials, and design. We negotiated over shapes—Kathy wanted round and curvy, but my experience and our budget screamed rectangular (I promised to build curves into the interior). And we saved our money so we could pay for the construction as we went.

"Of all the decisions we made about our home, the best by far was our decision to take our time in building. We had purchased a small ranch south of Durango, Colorado, and lived in a humble 900-square-foot house that was sixty years old. Though you literally had to step aside to let the other pass, at least we weren't in a camper on the job site. Kathy was reasonably comfortable and, therefore, immensely patient.

"In 2001, the foundation, footing, and underground infrastructure were put in on a site we'd chosen in the pinion and juniper woods on the ranch. When winter hit, we stopped. In the spring of 2002, my brother Ron moved into the tipi on the back of our property and helped me put up the walls and bond beam atop the straw. Then Gene Martinez hired on to help us with the roof framing. "You've got a complicated roof," the veteran carpenter told me weekly, if not daily. We pressed on through the fall and winter, building dormers, sheathing, felting, and finally getting the steel on top.

"We frequently had to melt the ice and snow off the 10/12 pitch with a propane weed burner before we could get started in the morning. The following May brought natural clay plaster to our straw walls below the conventional walls above. At last, I could fold up my tarps—we were officially dried in.

"Then the real work began. Cory Arellano, a wonderful craftsman, worked with me a solid year on interior framing, plumbing, electricity, insulation, drywall, plaster—if you build, you'll know the steps like the back of your hand. Though time marched on, thousands of dollars were saved in labor and contractor profit. And because we went slowly, Kathy and I changed virtually every wall except the wet walls as we grew comfortable in the space, anticipating our needs and wants. My original floor plan blueprint is worthless.

"David Drake, a fantastic detail craftsman on hiatus from emergency-room nursing, helped me put the finishing touches on our home in 2004. Now we're moved in, but I'll bet that even by this book's publication date, there are still dozens of jobs to finish on our home.

"Of course, I realize that we were lucky indeed that we didn't have to borrow money (at least not from a bank) and be chiseled into a 120-day completion schedule. Builder's wisdom states that there are three

A timber structure announces the entrance and provides cover for the external walkway. Dormers admit light and air into the bathroom.

Specifications	
Exterior Area:	3,070 Square Feet
Interior Area:	2,550 Square Feet
Designer/Architect:	Owners
Contractor/Builder:	Owners
Structural System:	Load Bearing or Post and Beam
Exterior Plaster:	Earthen Plaster
Interior Plaster:	Gypsum Plaster
Bales:	Wheat Straw Laid Flat

elements to building: time, cost efficiency, and quality—and you can only have control of two of the three. But I'd tell you that if you happen to be time wealthy, it seems you can purchase a little more of the other two. Get the Conditional Certificate of Occupancy, move in, and slow down when you get to the jobs that you will be looking at for the rest of your life. You won't regret it."

—Katherine and John

John and Katherine.

Stairs wrap around the wood-burning stove opposite the kitchen.

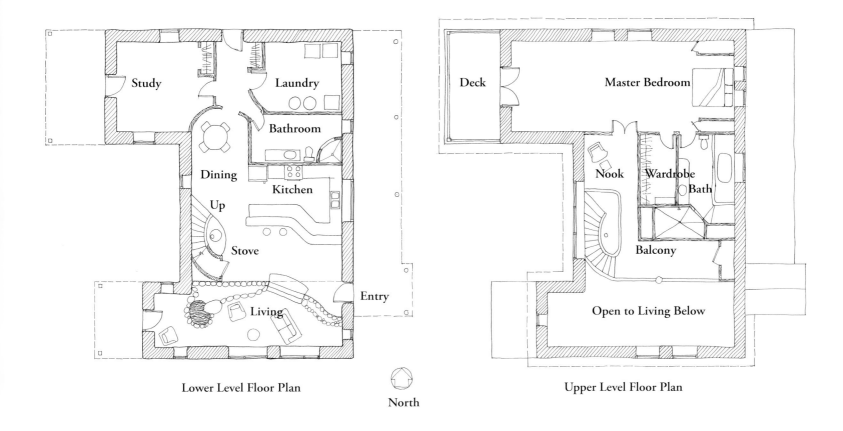

Lower Level Floor Plan

North

Upper Level Floor Plan

Curves within a Rectangular Plan

Katherine wanted curves and John wanted to keep the structure rectangular for construction ease. There is a nice blend of the two desires in the finished home. Their two-story house is an eclectic and very personal expression of things found and loved.

The step-down living space is passively heated with large south-facing windows the full two-story height with a cathedral ceiling. The kitchen and dining room are tucked under the second level and connected to the

upper level with stairs that artfully wrap around a traditional woodstove, which serves as their primary heating source.

The couple's study on the first floor also serves as the entertainment room and guest room. There is a bathroom on the first floor. The upper floor has a balcony that is open to and overlooks the living room. The couple's master suite includes a walk-in wardrobe next to the bath area, both off the master bedroom with a balcony looking west.

Extensive glazing on the south wall of the living space admits light deep into the house.

A cathedral ceiling above the living space with a second-story loft above the kitchen area.

46

A special Zen window, natural colors, indigenous tapestry art, and bottle ends in a curved plaster wall define the cozy dining area.

Strawbale, Cast-Earth, and Steel Home

Graybeal Residence • Carbondale, Colorado

Our Story

"We designed our home to take advantage of the sloping site and the outstanding southern views of the Elk Mountain Range. Our intent was to make our home as energy efficient and environmentally friendly as possible. The environmental impact of each building component was considered.

"The house is heated by passive solar energy with a little-used backup radiant heating system. The roof overhang and light shelf manage the seasonal change in the angle of the sun by allowing deep, penetrating heat in during the winter and excluding it from the space during the summer.

"During 90-degree summer days, the house maintains 73 to 76 degrees. We are able to manage this temperature using a combination of evening cross ventilation, the thermal mass of the floor, and a cast-earth wall. We installed solar panels to provide approximately 50 percent of the electrical needs of the house and two solar hot-water heaters to provide for our domestic needs.

"Our greenhouse provides us with fresh organic vegetables and fruit all year-round. We have planted the main roof with native grasses and flowers.

"We finished the exterior and interior of our strawbale walls with a breathable, dark earth-colored lime plaster. We anticipate that the roof and walls, which are sheathed with corrugated steel siding, will eventually patina to a similar color, both contrasting and blending with one another.

"We have selected interior materials from sustainable sources, such as plantation growth cherry for cabinetry, recycled Douglas fir for stairs, black steel with recycled content for accents, and countertops from North Dakota rather than Italy.

"We believe we have achieved a comfortable, beautiful, and healthy home from environmentally friendly materials, which matches our values for living lightly on the planet."

—Doug and Peggy

Steel siding clads the second-level offices, while lime-plastered strawbale walls surround the lower living level.

Specifications	
Exterior Area:	2,833 Square Feet
Interior Area:	2,463 Square Feet
Designer/Architect:	Doug Graybeal
Contractor/Builder:	Wolfe Brand Construction
Structural System:	Post and Beam
Exterior Plaster:	Lime with Integral Color
Interior Plaster:	Lime with Integral Color
Bales:	Two-String Wheat Straw Laid Flat with Bamboo Pinning

Peggy and Doug.

Contemporary Living with Natural Materials

The design is extremely well thought out and straight forward. Under a gently sloping shed roof are the kitchen, dining room, and living room. The master bedroom and walk-in wardrobe are separated by a fireplace and storage wall. A thick cast-earth wall separates these living spaces from service areas like the pantry, entryway, mechanical room, and bathrooms.

Above the service areas is a second story that houses two offices and an exercise room. This upper floor is sheathed with cold rolled, corrugated steel siding. The lower floor is wrapped with strawbales with a lime finish. Attached to the east is a greenhouse intended to provide year-round vegetables. The garage is separated from the living spaces by a sheathed wood-and-glass bridge.

The cast-earth wall is the most prominent feature in the living spaces with its earth textures fully expressed, a solid counterpoint to the full glazing on the south side. The cast-earth wall and concrete floors act as thermal mass to absorb solar gain from the south-facing windows and maintain an even interior temperature.

The entrance to the home is announced by a wood post-and-beam frame with a metal ceiling over the stairway.

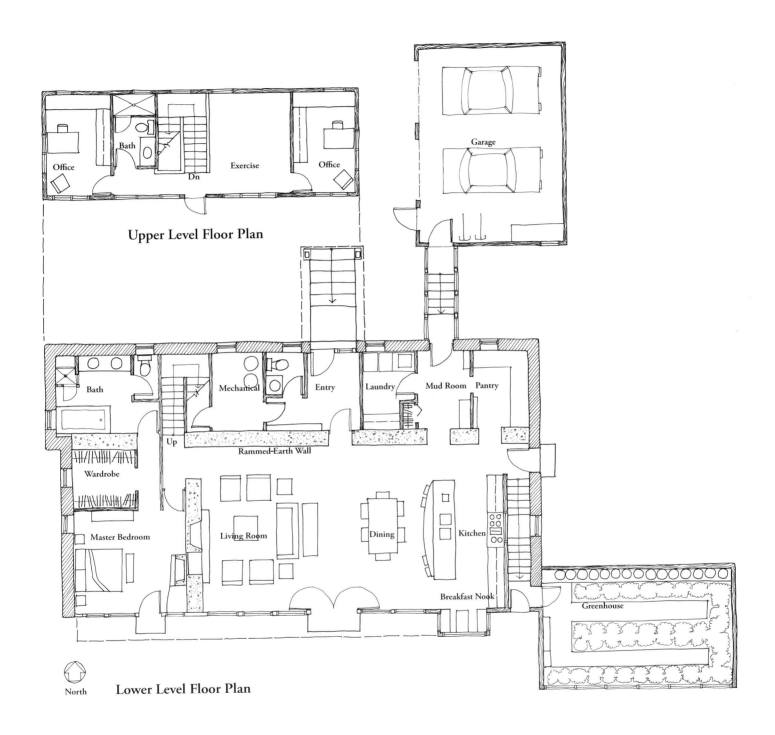

Upper Level Floor Plan

Office

Bath

Dn

Exercise

Office

Garage

Bath

Mechanical

Entry

Laundry

Mud Room

Pantry

Up

Rammed-Earth Wall

Wardrobe

Master Bedroom

Living Room

Dining

Kitchen

Breakfast Nook

Greenhouse

North

Lower Level Floor Plan

Paired, exposed wood beams and the wood deck of the shed roof cover the kitchen, dining, and living areas, with fireplace focus and cast-earth wall on the right.

Exposed beams rest on the cast-earth wall above a clean-lined, functional kitchen.

The master bedroom enjoys sunlight from the full-width windows. Soft butter yellow and white walls contrast with the exposed wood ceiling.

Solar panels for heating water and generating electricity are located on the office roof. Horizontal shades placed halfway up the windows provide shade and reflect light up to the interior ceiling.

Spectacular panoramic views are afforded by the windows and sliding-glass doors on either side of the kiva-style fireplace.

Family-Built Complex

Two Jacober Residences • Carbondale, Colorado

Our Story

"Our house project began when my four children and I bought five and a half acres of land near Carbondale, Colorado. Rio, Tai, and Forest, my three sons, and their father, Jock, had formed a construction company called Jacober Brothers Construction, specializing in green-building practices, especially strawbale buildings. They had recently finished building a really beautiful strawbale house for Jock near Glenwood Springs and were working on several other projects throughout the Roaring Fork Valley.

"We secured a great construction loan, which, combined with the expertise of Jacober Brothers, allowed us to build two beautiful houses for our family. My son Rio and his wife, Robin, live in the additional dwelling unit with their two children, Wilder and Montana. My youngest son, Forest, lives in his apartment downstairs in the big house. Tai, his wife, Molly, and their daughter, Phia, visit a lot, and my daughter Sierra is here often. Both houses are filled with love and laughter, and every single morning I wake up full of gratitude and appreciation for the beauty that surrounds me.

"Forest originally designed the big house, which is not really big, and Rio designed the smaller house. We wanted to build houses that looked like they had been here for a century, with classic lines and materials. We are all believers that small is beautiful and tried to build accordingly.

"We were committed to using the greenest materials we could find. Jacober Brothers Construction is strongly dedicated to minimizing waste at all their project sites and this place was no exception. We threw no wood in the dumpster, and we are still burning scrap pieces of lumber in our fireplace. Both houses are located to maximize sun exposure and the passive solar design is so efficient that our houses use very little additional heat (which is radiant-floor heat powered by propane), even here in the Colorado Rockies where temperatures can drop below zero at night for weeks at a time. All the exposed wood, including the trusses, cabinets, and stair treads, is recycled Douglas fir from mills in the Northwest.

"The floors are concrete and bamboo. Almost all the walls and ceilings were hand worked with Diamond plaster. Rugs and furniture are all natural fibers, such as leather, wool, and cotton. Every surface in both houses has been rubbed by the hands of those I love so the walls glow with a warmth and patina that cannot be attained without hard work and careful attention."

—Francie and Forest, Rio and Robin

Specifications		
Francie and Forest's Home		**Rio and Robin's Home**
Exterior Area:	2,597 Square Feet	825 Square Feet
Interior Area:	2,130 Square Feet	698 Square Feet
Designer / Architect:	Jacober Brothers Construction	
Contractor / Builder:	Jacober Brothers Construction	
Structural System:	Post and Beam	
Exterior Plaster:	Cement Stucco Hand Applied over Chicken Wire and Metal Lath with Trowels	
Interior Plaster:	Gypsum Plaster Hand Applied over Chicken Wire and Metal Lath with Trowels	
Bales:	Wheat and Oat Straw Laid Flat with Internal Rebar and Bamboo Pins	

Francie and Forest's Floor Plan

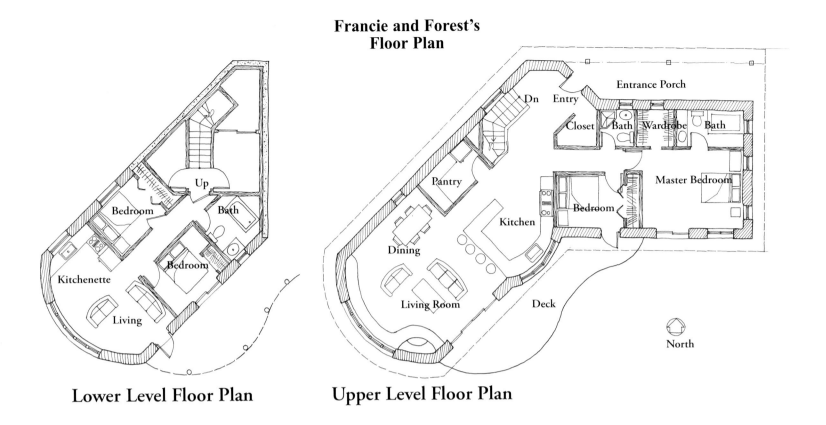

Lower Level Floor Plan

Upper Level Floor Plan

North

Francie and Forest's Home

Francie and her son Forest live in the house along a flower-sided pathway to the west of the family property. It is part single story and part two story due to the change in grade. Francie lives on the upper level that includes her bedroom wing, kitchen, dining, and living spaces. Forest occupies the bedroom, living, and bathing quarters in the walkout basement below.

There are fantastic views of Mt. Sopris from the kitchen and through sliding doors in the living space. The curved end of the living space is anchored by a kiva-style fireplace and wraparound windows with knockout views of the valley below.

Visible above the kitchen and living area are large timber frame trusses made from recycled wood from Pacific Northwest mills. Area rugs are placed on stained concrete floors throughout the home. Soft off-white colors create a light-filled atmosphere.

Francie and Forest's covered entrance porch.

Multilevel Country Homes

Soft-colored walls create a warm ambiance in Francie's bedroom. Niches and deep windowsills, hallmarks of straw-bale building, are also beautifully incorporated.

Recycled wood trusses define the cathedral ceiling over the kitchen, dining, and living areas of Francie and Forest's home.

Multilevel Country Homes

Clerestory monitors rise above the roof of Rio and Robin's home, bringing light into the center of the space.

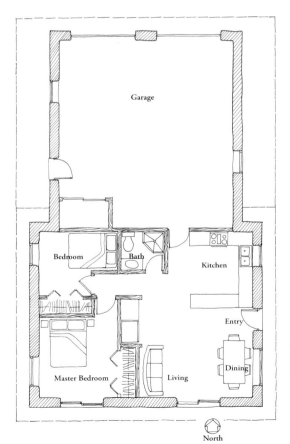

**Rio and Robin's
Floor Plan**

North

Rio and Robin's Home

Two houses on one lot. Both are strawbale: one for single mother Francie and son Forest and one for her son Rio and his family. Both are designed and built by Jacober Brothers Construction. Rio and Forest are, along with father Jock Jacober, Jacober Brothers Construction. So the houses are both owner built and contractor built.

Rio and Robin's house is a single-story T-shaped building with garage and storage in the north wing and living quarters to the south, with ample solar gain and views of Mt. Sopris. Its most prominent feature is the raised clerestory lighting structure for both the garage and living wings. Generous overhangs with gutters and downspouts conduct moisture away from the plastered bale walls.

The sloping site allows for a single-story, south-facing main living level. The multilevel north face, on the opposite page, shows how the building accommodates the sloping site.

Multilevel Home Stepping Down a Slope

O'Kane-Jacober Residence • Glenwood Springs, Colorado

Our Story

"When the Roaring Fork Valley became home to our family about ten years ago, Lynette, as if by fate, discovered an affordable lot with a mountain stream flowing through it. Intrigued with the strawbale construction process, we had worked as volunteers on the Waldorf School buildings in our area. I had been a builder for years, and Lynette was an artist who needed a studio. The strawbale infill house we designed gave us an aesthetic home, fulfilled our family's needs, and provided the opportunity to participate in the building process.

"Early in the planning process, we established basic design criteria. These dealt with our lifestyle, our aesthetic choices, the local housing market, and our complicated hillside site. The result is a house that can literally be divided into three distinct family living spaces, has access to the earth on four of the five levels, is not isolated from the creek, and remains unobtrusive in scale when approached at the main entry.

"From the outset of the construction process, we pursued a casual approach. I would alternately hire available young labor or my own college-age children to work on the project. During the summer and on vacations, they pitched in, and slowly the home grew to be habitable. The building is a post-and-beam structure with strawbale infill.

The strawbales are placed on edge, slightly increasing the interior square footage.

"Because of the hillside, the ground floors are wood joists on stem walls. The foundation is comprised of insulated concrete forms. The cathedral roof of the main room is made of structural insulated panels. We had some luck obtaining interior and exterior doors from misorders at local suppliers. A design criteria was to utilize as many real materials as possible—steel, wood, concrete, plasters, and stone—and obtain these from as local a source as possible. The result has been modest finishes, all of which have been done on-site with our own hands and the hands of our children and workers.

"To us, the journey is the important part of building a home. We want our home to have the inherent qualities of strength, balance, security, warmth, and hospitality. The hearths are the centers of this good energy. At the foundation of the fireplace is a flat rock, too large and imbedded to have been moved from its location. Upon this rock, Lynette painted an anatomical heart. If, in some future world, it sees the light of day again, then the house will be gone. Until then, it beats metaphorically, sustaining the life of a true home."

—Lynette and Jock

Specifications	
Exterior Area:	3,450 Square Feet
Interior Area:	2,970 Square Feet
Designer/Architect:	O'Kane-Jacober
Contractor/Builder:	Jacober Brothers Construction
Structural System:	Post and Beam
Exterior Plaster:	Cement Stucco
Interior Plaster:	Gypsum
Bales:	Wheat Bales on Edge

Multiunit, Multilevel Creekside Home

How do you step a strawbale home down a slope? The O'Kane-Jacober residence utilizes several floor levels separated by one-half-floor height, and pin wheeling around the central stairway. From the south entrance and living room floor, there appears to be one low-hipped roof story, while the north side has three stories. It is surprising to see how much the building changes appearance as one walks around it. Rooms on the east side overlook a creek and north-facing windows overlook the canyon with the creek.

The rooms in the house are appropriately scaled and comfortable, with a cozy furniture arrangement and a high-efficiency Rumford fireplace in the center. Light is usually brought in through two sides of each room. A mix of wood and stained concrete floors combined with white, curved plaster walls and wood ceilings adds to the warm ambiance.

The house is designed to have several self-contained apartments with separate entrances for extended family or guests.

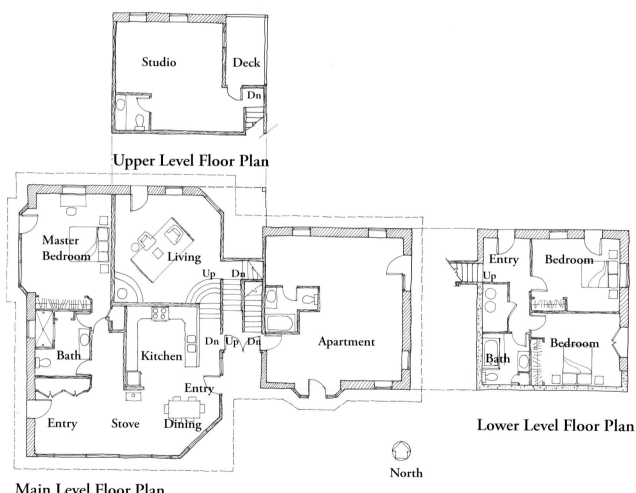

Upper Level Floor Plan

Main Level Floor Plan

Lower Level Floor Plan

North

The Rumford fireplace provides a warm focal point to the living room, with its wood beams and bead board ceiling, softly curved thick walls, and wood floor.

A hipped bead board ceiling graces the softly lit master bedroom.

Strong horizontal lines are created with the concrete counter and exposed shelving.

Sophisticated Artistry
in a Building Cluster

Villafranco Residence • Carbondale, Colorado

Our Story

"It started (and ended) with the aesthetic. In between, we grew to appreciate the efficiencies and functionalities of strawbale, but we would be lying if we did not admit that it has been mostly about beauty. We had been vacationing in Colorado, visiting Sarah's family for years. At the conclusion of our trips, we always had this empty feeling about leaving. One trip we simply asked each other, 'Why not live here?' That started the ball rolling.

"With Sarah's medical residency in Washington, D.C., to complete, we had plenty of time to find the right piece of land and consider design elements. It was something that we worked on to some degree every day for nearly four years. It became an artistic expression that allowed us to draw on creativities that have no connection to our professional lives.

"Almost everyone who worked on our house recognized its unique character and extended themselves to achieve the result. Our design and construction architects (same firm), interior designer, and builder all bought into the concept from the very beginning and their performance underscored the importance of surrounding yourself with highly regarded professionals who understand and share your special intentions.

"We have been city dwellers, so we have attempted to incorporate the edge and clean lines of modern urban design with the warmth and beauty of the walls. The lime walls, with their variety of finishes and extensive color palette, are the stars of the show. The introduction of a variety of metals in every room serves as cold counter balance to the warmth of the walls, giving the house a contemporary feel that is less common in strawbale homes. The combination inspires a physical effect: relaxed but sharp and sophisticated.

"We wanted plenty of space so that we could have room for our immediate family and for guests, but we did not want a large house. With our architect's direction, we settled on a design that had more of a feel of a compound with transitional spaces both inside and outside. We also thought a lot about stairs: how they feel on your feet, what you see as you climb them, and whether they might serve as a gathering place or a sculptural element.

"We never considered the decks to be optional. They were necessary to bring the outside in and to maintain the horizontal and vertical rhythm of the property itself, which steps up steeply from the Crystal River below, forms a mesa, and heads up again to the ridge behind the property.

"In selecting Jeff as our architect, we committed to sustainable and energy-efficient design. The structure itself is a combination of steel and reclaimed beams. Jeff placed it perfectly for passive solar gain and

South view showing two of the three buildings. The guest quarters on the left are connected to the three-story main living quarters in the center.

Specifications	
Exterior Area:	4,719 Square Feet
Interior Area:	3,868 Square Feet
Architect:	Jeff Dickinson, Donna Riley
Interior Designer:	Tami Kupper
Contractor/Builder:	Cole West Corporation
Structural System:	Post and Beam
Exterior Plaster:	Lime Plaster Applied by Machine and Finished by Hand
Interior Plaster:	Lime Plaster Applied by Machine and Finished by Hand
Bales:	Wheat Bales Laid Flat, Pinned with Bamboo

A large window above the cooktop affords mountain views. A recycled wood floor extends down one step to the dining space to the right.

orientation to the western slope of Mt. Sopris, which is so present that it feels unreal and two dimensional, like a perfect mural. The most beautiful and largest beams are hand-hewn Douglas fir, straight from a Cleveland automotive plant that had been disassembled. The floors are reclaimed white pine and elm or cast concrete. The roof is recycled copper, which was as cheap as galvanized steel. We also made sure to involve a number of local artists and artisans to provide that last bit of local character that ties the house even tighter to the community: a reclaimed mahogany door with hand-carved Love-in-the-Mist flower, reclaimed ash-and-walnut tables, steelwork by a local blacksmith, custom-made glass light fixtures, and so on.

"We chose lime plaster for its breathability and improved perform-ance (less cracking), but most of all for the varied and vivid colors that could be achieved. The lime plaster caused us the most stress and now provides the most pleasure. There are very few people who work with lime plaster in this country and the work is made more complicated by combining bale walls with some interior drywall. With lime, we were able to achieve tranquil blues, powerful earthy greens, creamy yellows and oranges, chocolaty browns, and a metallic red. We transitioned between smooth and rough finishes and anchored the whole thing with a three-story earth wall that provides visual continuity and mass.

"We sought out strong personalities as contributors, which presented unique challenges at times as creative minds wrestled with all sorts of issues, most notably the combination of materials to obtain the desired effect. There were days when the debate between right and left brainers was loud and full of friction, but that tension provided a better result."

—John and Sarah

The hallway to the main-level guest
room leads through multicolored
arches.

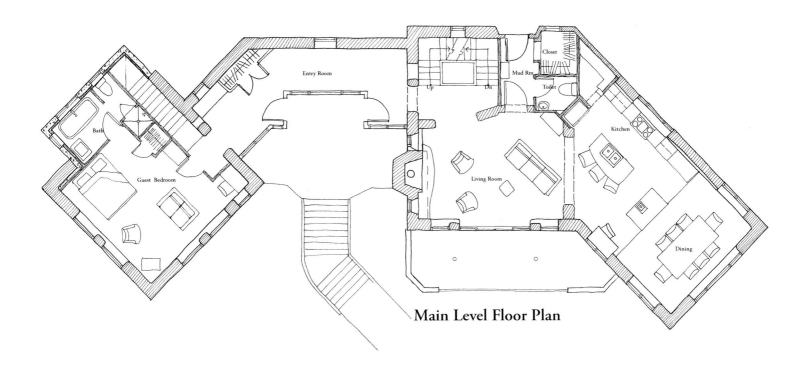

Main Level Floor Plan

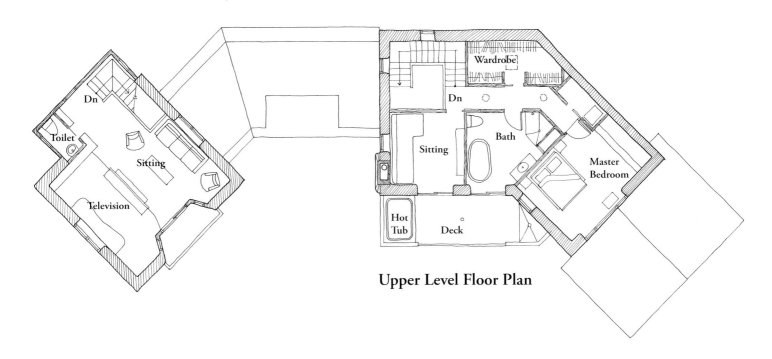

Upper Level Floor Plan

Multilevel Country Homes

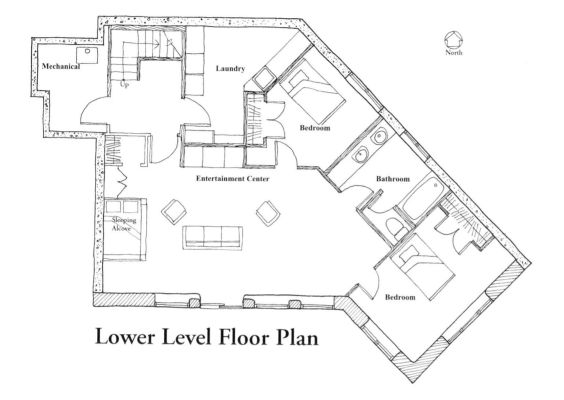

Lower Level Floor Plan

Mechanical

Laundry

Up

North

Bedroom

Entertainment Center

Bathroom

Sleeping Alcove

Bedroom

The dining area has a cathedral ceiling, warm colors, and spectacular mountain views.

Compound of Buildings on the Mountainside

What started as a grass roots owner-builder movement to construct a simple, small, inexpensive shelter has evolved into a sophisticated, artistic, finely finished expression in the Villafranco residence. John and Sarah were not going to design and build it themselves, so they sought out an architect who shared their vision of a beautiful, sustainable residence and contractors who had the skills to transform that vision into this artistic expression.

Luckily, there are architects and skilled craftspeople who have

obtained the training, skills, vision, and experience to be able to respond to a couple who had a dream. Owners who prefer to work in this manner today are able to find those with whom they can fulfill their objectives.

All the required functions, including living, sleeping, entertaining, and guest quarters, are not contained within a large single building, but instead are separated and distributed into three distinct structures that flow down the east-facing slope of the mountain and are arranged for maximum solar gain.

The office space and entertainment room are combined yet separated by a TV nook in this soft-colored room.

Lime plaster finishes used throughout the house demonstrate the wide range of colors and finishes available with this versatile material.

View of house from the southeast. The curved roof extends over the south-facing windows to provide shade in the summer.

Playful Home Amid
Red Rock Castles

Wentz-Messick Residence • Southern Utah

Our Story

"My initial reaction to strawbale structures was that I could never build one due to my allergies. But the pictures in the first strawbale book by Bill and Athena Steen, *The Straw Bale House*, kept calling me, and I decided to go to one of their workshops in southern Arizona. I spent the week with my head in strawbale and never sneezed. So my excuse was gone, and I was hooked.

"I bought an empty lot and put up a Pacific Domes 16-foot canvas dome. Mike and I lived in that for three years while getting a well, phone service, and electricity, and building a studio. We did a lot of the work on the studio ourselves. Two guys in our valley put up the framing, roof, and windows, and an electrician did the wiring. We did everything else from the plumbing, bales, ceiling, and plastering to the floors.

"After three years spent on the studio, we went right into building the house, only this time we decided to speed up the process with more help.

Julie and Mike.

Our builder was with us from start to finish as well as a number of other people coming and going for certain jobs. All but three of the people who worked on our house live in the same small valley. Our choice of a builder was the best decision we made. Also, living on the property and building the studio helped us fine-tune the house design, which continually changed over a four-year period.

"Mike and I put the bales up, but this time when it came time for plastering, we held a plaster party. We called and emailed a number of people but figured we'd be pretty lucky if anyone aside from our reliable and supportive moms came. The first weekend we had about sixteen people show up. Some people called the night before to see if they could come. Some of them we didn't even know. We plastered three times as much as we had hoped to. The second weekend we had almost as many people.

"Both weekends left us blown away by the amount of work accomplished and emotionally overwhelmed by the support, effort, and time that our friends and family had given to us. It's fantastic what people will do when you just ask or put the word out.

"While we were often overwhelmed by the project, we still managed to get in all the details that we feel make our home ours. We incorporated a number of things we've collected over the years directly into the walls and doors. The home has a happy, comfortable feel, and I don't think we'd change a thing if we had it to do over.

Specifications	
Exterior Area:	1,175 Square Feet
Interior Area:	947 Square Feet
Designer/Architect:	Susie Harrington and Kalen Jones
Contractor/Builder:	Owner
Structural System:	Post and Beam
Exterior Plaster:	Earthen Plaster Applied by Hand
Interior Plaster:	Earthen Plaster Applied by Hand
Bales:	Wheat Bales Laid Flat with Bamboo External Pins

"Extensive research was needed to find the natural materials for our home. We used reed mats and tongue-and-groove wood for ceilings. We used cork flooring in the yoga loft and bedroom, recycled tile in the bathroom, and earth floors in the rest of the house. Our walls are plastered with earth and then finished with a combination of gypsum, clay, mica, wheat-paste plaster, and milk paints. Whenever possible, we used nontoxic stains, sealers, and so on, which required a lot of Internet ordering and planning ahead. We have a solar hot-water heater with a tankless Rinai heater as a backup. So far the design of the house is working wonderfully, and we are looking forward to winter to see how warm and cozy it stays."

—Julie and Mike

Carved hearts on custom-made door to bedroom.

74

Whimsical Strawbale

Whimsical comes to mind when you experience Julie and Mike's new home. Whoever thought of putting a slippery slide from the meditation/yoga loft to the center of the living room? It's fun. Notice the curved stonework carried all across the kitchen from window to cabinet. The windowsills flow, with hand-placed stonework, down the walls. The bedroom door is custom made with two carved hearts.

Yet the house is a rather sophisticated passive solar design by Susie Harrington and Kalen Jones. The home is long in the east-west direction with ample glazing to the south. West and north windows are minimized to reduce afternoon glare and heat loss. All living spaces are on the main floor except the meditation/yoga loft, which has clerestory windows and magnificent views of the valley to the south. It is a modest, small house, sensibly laid out but with enough creative expression and personality to not feel banal.

Earthen floors, earthen plaster walls, and curved reed-mat ceilings express a naturalness, a handmade palette of materials that combine to give an elegant, open feeling.

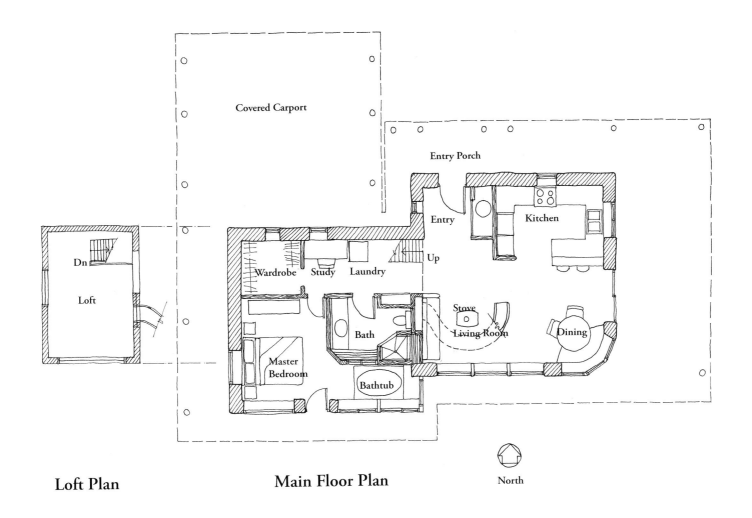

Loft Plan

Main Floor Plan

North

A curved slippery slide flows from the meditation/yoga loft to the center of the living room. On the right, there are a built-in couch, gas stove, and hall to the bedroom.

Multilevel Country Homes

The stairway to the meditation loft has a painting as the focal point. Niches in the strawbale wall are to the right.

The kitchen features many unique items, including a reed-mat ceiling, river pebbles carried through the window, plaster walls, wood cabinets, and an earthen floor.

A shed roof addition to the original gable-roofed house provides space for the home-owners' growing family.

Modest Home Expanded for a Growing Family

McIntyre Residence • Raymond, Nebraska

Our Story

"I did the design for both the house and addition—the house in spring and summer of 1995, the addition in spring of 2003. Kim and I were the builders for everything except the well and septic system, hardwood floor, and carpet installations. We started construction (grading and footings) on September 1, 1995, and moved in the day after Thanksgiving in 1997.

"I continued to work full-time during the construction, so our building was done mostly evenings and weekends. I did use about a month of vacation over the two years we were building. We didn't get power out to the site until about a month after the house was closed in (roof on, windows and doors in, partial first exterior plaster coat on).

"Our bales were locally produced poly-tied wheat straw. We didn't have them baled specifically for building, but we bought about 10 percent more than we needed for the walls and our original living roof and picked the tightest bales for the walls. They are pretty uniform in size, 38 inches long, 18 inches deep, and 14 inches high (oriented with the strings in the plane of the wall). Pinning is #4 rebar. Bales are spaced off the concrete footings with insulated sill plates.

"We used post-and-beam construction. Interior posts, floor joists, exposed ceiling beams, and planks are all locally cut cottonwood (8 x 8 inch and 4 x 8 inch). Posts in the walls are plywood and lumber built to the same thickness as the bales (18 inches). Roof rafters and interior wall framing are standard dimensional lumber.

"Interior plaster is Structolite (commercial bagged gypsum-perlite mix). We used two to three coats over the straw and one coat over a base coat of drywall compound on the framed interior walls (to match the straw wall texture). All were hand applied and hand finished with sponges to smooth out trowel marks and leave a rounded, pebbly surface. We experimented with various mixes and found that the lightweight, sticky Structolite worked best in the window-opening arches. It also created a quieter, less echo-y surface than the gypsum sand and lime sand mixes we tried.

"Exterior plaster is a lime-Portland-sand mix made on-site. Proportions varied a bit, but 2:1:5 is pretty representative. We decided to add some Portland cement to the mix because of the exposure on the east and west walls, and we weren't sure that a lime sand mix would stand up

Scott and Kim.

Specifications	
Exterior Area:	1,433 Square Feet
Interior Area:	1,212 Square Feet
Designer/Architect:	Scott McIntyre
Contractor/Builder:	Kim and Scott McIntyre
Structural System:	Post and Beam Locally Grown Cottonwood
Exterior Plaster:	Lime, Cement, and Sand Applied with Trowels
Interior Plaster:	Structolite Applied with Trowels
Bales:	Wheat Straw Tied with Polypropylene

to our weather. We used two undercoats (mixed with gray Portland and a final coat using white Portland and powdered pigment. The white Portland was a much nicer mix to work with—there were virtually no check cracks. The cost for the white cement was about four times higher than the gray, but we only used a couple of bags for the full final coat so it didn't amount to much additional expense. We used it for all the coats when we built our greenhouse a few years ago. All the exterior plaster was applied (troweled) by hand and finished by hand. We wore through several pairs of fuzzy cotton work gloves to smooth away the trowel marks as the plaster was setting up."

—Kim and Scott

The woodstove is surrounded by cob walls that absorb heat and slowly radiate it into the living space.

Cozy, Handmade Family Home

We were particularly impressed with the coziness and handmade character of this lovely small home. There is no wasted space and each area is clearly delineated. The kitchen is open to the dining room and living room, allowing easy conversation during meal preparation. The thermal-mass wall surrounding the wood-burning stove absorbs and radiates the heat, making the temperature more even throughout the day.

The original house had a living roof over the south-facing living area.

Larger beams were used to carry the additional load. As the homeowners' children grew older and needed private space, a second-level shed roof addition was built above the living and dining space. The new addition blends with the original house in a very clear and comfortable way.

Unostentatious, modest, and sensitively sited, the McIntyre home is a complement to the site and their family.

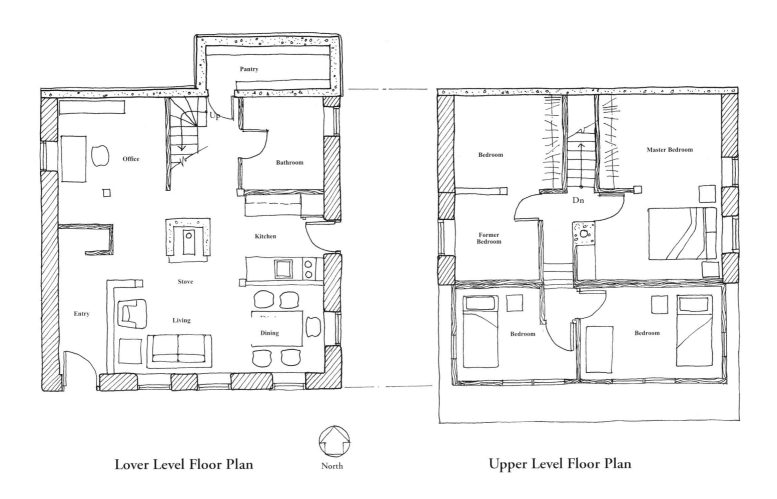

Lover Level Floor Plan

North

Upper Level Floor Plan

A view from the living room toward the woodstove, kitchen, and dining room. The kitchen has a lower ceiling that supports the master bedroom above. Open shelving and simple cabinetry add to the charm of the house.

Multilevel Country Homes

The living and dining areas have a heavy timbered ceiling that supported a living roof prior to the construction of the new addition.

Quaint home featuring one and one half levels with shed dormers on the upper level. The living room balcony is on the right. Solar panels are located above the dormer.

Earthly Dwelling of the Feminine Divine

van Balen Residence • Carson, New Mexico

My Story

"This is a woman's story—a feminine perspective.

"In May of 1991, my daughter, Molly, and I took a painting class in northern New Mexico where we camped out and painted the landscapes. My spirit soared in this new environment.

"That October my mother sent me a check for $5,000, thanking me for the time she had lived with us ten years prior. I used the money to buy ten acres of land bordering the Carson National Forest out in the middle of nowhere. The realtor said, "If you can find this land, I'll help you buy it. A twin check followed. I used the second check to buy a used Toyota truck.

"My next challenge was to find a way to live on the land. I saw an article on strawbale houses in a Santa Fe newspaper. There were workshops being offered in Santa Fe on this innovative process. The thought of living in a straw nest—ah, that beat pitching a tent. The proposed cost was $30 a square foot. That seemed workable.

"In Taos, Molly and I met Tomas and his partner, Tom Lamb. They had built a strawbale house in Canada. Tomas and Tom put together a plan for a story-and-a-half house measuring 24 x 40 feet. They would prepare the timbers for a post-and-beam structure and complete the foundation for $12,000, including the pad for a masonry stove. This quote far exceeded my budget. I still wonder why I proceeded. That year the state gave twelve strawbale building permits. I also had no blueprint.

"In January of 1992, I was diagnosed with colon cancer. I had surgery but when chemotherapy and radiation were prescribed, I spurned the prescription. My intuition told me that building a home in the forest would be my therapy. I wondered if I would even be around the next year for a permit, so I decided to go ahead without one.

"Honoring my process and becoming self-sufficient became the catalyst for living my dream and gave me the courage to proceed. Now I speak from experience when I tell my children or anyone who will listen, 'If you have a dream, the universe will support it.'

"My husband, Mike, came to help clear a road to the site and my three sons, Sean, Seamus, and Peter, all working in construction, took a two-week vacation to put up the timbers and cover the roof with plywood. "My other daughters, Siobhan and Sarah, with Sarah's friend John, cooked our food, documented the story on canvas, and cheered us on. We named the home Shekinah, a Hebrew word that means "the earthly dwelling of the feminine divine." Shekinah took the shape of a cathedral in the pinion forest.

Specifications	
Exterior Area:	1,920 Square Feet
Interior Area:	1,628 Square Feet
Designer/Architect:	Owner
Contractor/Builder	Family and Friends
Structural System:	Post and Beam
Exterior Plaster:	Cement Plaster on Chicken Wire
Interior Plaster:	Cement Plaster on Chicken Wire
Bales:	Two-String Wheat Laid Flat with Rebar Pins

"Strawbale building was a new phenomenon in the neighborhood, so part of the early process involved putting out fear fires and giving out facts as I learned them. The men in the neighborhood who were experienced builders and had built their own alternative homes were happy to have work. They came with their tools and we proceeded, wrapping the timbers in woven wire, setting the strawbales against the wire, and insulating the roof under the steel panels.

"Because I didn't get a bank loan, we didn't have to deal with bank regulations, which freed up our schedule. It was only by the many intelligent suggestions of those involved and by the grace of God that Shekinah evolved into an environmentally sound home.

"The wheat strawbales from Colorado were approximately 14 x 36 inches. Putting them against the woven wire made for a smooth exterior wall. They were pinned with rebar. The inside walls were covered with chicken wire. Molly chose the windows and Tom Lamb designed the splays. His presence, wisdom, and experience were tremendous factors in our success.

"Splitting bales, shaving them to fit, and sewing the exterior and interior wires together with twine was tedious work. With scaffolding, the exterior walls were plastered by many hands. After camping out all summer, we moved into the upper floor in October.

"The entire community of friends and neighbors helped. Alan brought the recipe from Hollywood for the interior plaster. Parker supervised the installation of the photovoltaic panels. Albie Barden came from Maine to build the masonry stove. David built the cistern to catch the rainwater and melting snow. He also made the Japanese bath. Larry laid out the laterals; Mike and I laid the brick floor. Scott was there through it all with his down-to-earth philosophy and good humor.

"Shekinah took form as the money became available. A screened-in porch was added to the north. My family came often. One summer they built a portal on the east and a hefty table from the scraps.

"On completion, the total cost was $50 a square foot. Another blessing was that I lived there on this sacred land for $100 a month. This included water, wood, electricity, and taxes.

"Shekinah inspired our creativity, challenged relationships, endeared the process and product to the point that many other strawbale homes in Carson followed. Shekinah was a family and community affair. We all lived, loved, learned, and celebrated the miracle. After my children left New Mexico, I left, too. I cried when I left Shekinah. She is truly a spiritual nest."

—JoAn

JoAn.

A view from the entry to the dining area. The stairway to the second floor recalls JoAn's trip to Greece. Tall windows bring in south and west light to the dining area, which is paved with bricks.

Strawbale Nest in the Forest

This is the strawbale home that lit our fire. While exploring natural building we had visited adobe, rammed earth, earth ships, and clay/straw buildings and had less than satisfactory reactions. We spent the night here with the outside temperature at 27 degrees and were very comfortable in the morning with the masonry heater still warm from the evening firing. Our natural building direction was set. We have continued to be involved in the design and construction of strawbale homes since 1998—including one for ourselves.

JoAn's objective in constructing this 2,000-square-foot home was to build within her means and live on her $575-per-month social security income. The home is totally off-grid, with rainwater catchment, photovoltaic cells, and a septic system. There is a need to bring propane gas periodically for cooking purposes. Kitchen, dining, bathing, and bedroom are on the main level. Along with the living space on the second floor, with a balcony overlooking the forest beyond, there are also two small bedrooms and a small bath.

Tall windows and white walls give a bright feeling to the home. An eclectic mix of salvaged and collected furniture graces the home and gives it a timeless quality.

Though she has since moved from Shekinah because of health reasons, JoAn conducted life quite comfortably and lived within her means at Shekinah.

A view from the dining area through lace curtains to the entry and the wall of the bathing room, with a mural painted by one of JoAn's daughters.

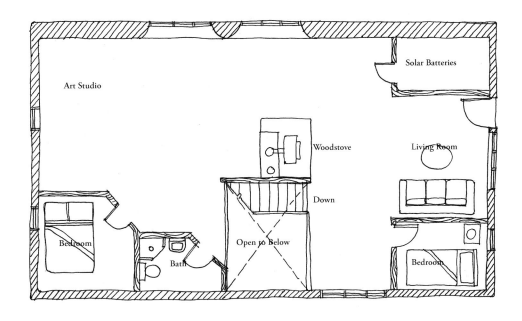

Upper Level Floor Plan

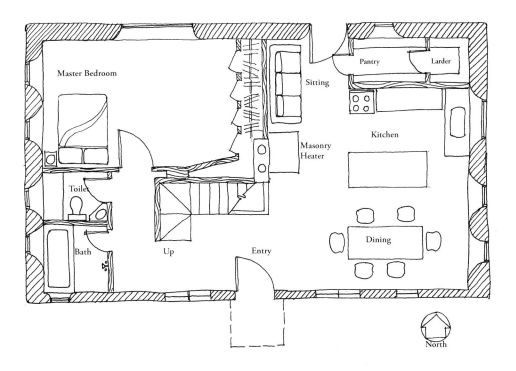

Lower Level Floor Plan

Multilevel Country Homes

Southeast view of home showing new sunroom, wraparound porch, and patio additions. The water and photovoltaic panels are angled to take advantage of the low winter sun.

Off-Grid Mountain Home

Charette Residence • Teton Valley, Idaho

My Story

"I came from Maine to Jackson Hole to ski and bike. Living in apartments and making bagels worked for a while, but I wanted a place of my own. I worked construction and started accumulating materials that were castoffs or unused but still good.

"I located a beautiful site in the foothills of the Teton Mountains overlooking Teton Valley, Idaho. I utilized a simple shed roof design with living spaces on the first level and a bedroom and meditation room in a loft. Since there are significant roof loads, I used large timbers for structure and wrapped the strawbale wall around the frame.

"I would work during the winter months to acquire money and materials and build during the summer months. I did most of the work myself, sometimes with the help of friends. I was able to build the house with scrounged materials with the cash flow generated from construction labor; however, I did need to take a small mortgage to handle some of the larger costs that were incurred.

"The house is a couple of miles from the nearest county road and there were no utilities available, so my house is entirely off-grid. I collect rainwater and store it in concrete cisterns on the north of the building, filtering it for all domestic purposes. Power and hot-water panels are on the roof.

"The south-facing two stories initially took the brunt of the weather, so I decided to add a sunroom and a wraparound porch. They provide additional passive heat to the home in the winter and outdoor living space off the living room in the summer. They have reduced the amount of wall exposed to rain and snow."

—Brian

Specifications	
Exterior Area:	1,008 Square Feet
Interior Area:	835 Square Feet
Designer/Architect:	Brian Charette
Contractor/Builder:	Owner
Structural System:	Post and Beam
Exterior Plaster:	Lime-and-Cement Plaster Applied by Hand
Interior Plaster:	Gypsum Plaster Applied by Hand
Bales:	Wheat Bales Laid Flat with Rebar Internal Pins

The loft sitting and meditation area, with windows to the
east and sunroom to the right. The chokecherry stairway
to the left leads down to the living/dining area.

Multilevel Country Homes

Bachelor Strategy for Independent Living

This is how a young man with some construction experience—scrounging materials from buildings that were being demolished or remodeled, utilizing materials he harvested on-site—built his dream. He collected windows that were rejected, wood that wasn't going to be used, and kitchen cabinets that had a former life, and then organized them into a comfortable home.

The entry, kitchen, study, dining room, and living room are open with stairs leading up to the loft meditation room and master bedroom. The bathroom and utility rooms are on the main floor. Large, exposed post-and-beam logs articulate the space. Brian built the stairway with cordwood. He set short wood logs in a cement mortar and wrapped native chokecherry wood steps around a central post. The stiles and handrail are also chokecherry.

The house is entirely off-grid. Water is heated in a roof-mounted solar panel and goes to storage tanks in the utility room. Photovoltaic panels are mounted for maximum winter efficiency on the roof and provide all power for the house. The passive solar orientation is enhanced by the addition of a new two-story sunroom and wraparound porch that protect the south side from the prevailing weather.

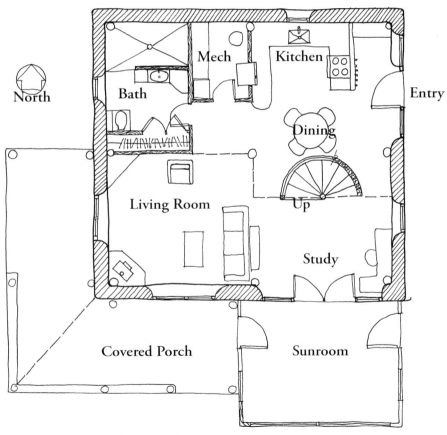

Floor Plan

View looking down into the kitchen from the loft through the chokecherry stairway and handrail, both handcrafted by Brian.

View looking from the living room toward the central cordwood stair, with the kitchen and study beyond. Large log construction provides a masculine strength to the building.

Chokecherry harvested from the site was used for the stairs and handrails. The outer support for the stairs is made with cordwood logs mortared with ends exposed.

95

SMALL-TOWN DREAM HOMES

A view from the south at twilight. Windows, protected from the high summer sun by curved roof overhangs, allow deep sunlight penetration during the winter months.

Curvaceous, Passive Solar Home

Harrington-Jones Residence • Moab, Utah

Our Story

"As ecological designers we were committed to making our home as sustainable as possible, which to us meant passive solar strawbale with natural finishes. We also wanted it to showcase ideas we are not always able to express so clearly in other's houses, which included harmonizing with the landscape, creating a sense of either enclosure or transparency, depending on the weather, and making it as small as possible without sacrificing beauty or function.

"The secluded yet cheap lot we found within biking distance of town is on a north-facing hillside. Balancing views with the desire for solar access drove the design. By staggering the house in three blocks, the dramatic east and west views are available from several rooms, with the exception of a bathtub alcove that proved too complex for its ultimate benefit. Although this complexity did add cost, we feel it was worth it.

"We originally thought we would have a living roof. Concerns that it would use undue water in the desert, and our affinity for the organic shake work on Bart Prince's houses led us in a different direction. We modeled the roof on the computer for assembly out of factory-built trusses, and roofed it with recycled plastic 'shakes.'

"One of our favorite spots, the built-in bench around the woodstove, almost didn't happen. We had not planned on having a woodstove, but Susie fell in love with one at a recycling yard late in the design process. Similarly, we chose a ground-source heat pump for our backup heat source when we realized that the utility trench could accommodate the ground loop without too much additional cost. It is connected to radiant tubing in the adobe floor, which we use for both heating and cooling. However, the cooling load at the height of summer is too high and an evaporative-air cooler would be better suited to the demand.

"Upon arrival, the wheat strawbales looked golden, but sampling with a moisture probe revealed excess dampness. An isolated thunderstorm had soaked them the night before they were loaded onto the trailer for delivery. We were able to exchange them for dry oat strawbales; unfortunately, the mice loved the softer straw and plentiful grain that was still attached.

"We acted as the general contractors, but we had plenty of skilled help. Building forced us to find ways to deal with stress and learn to work together to address the never-ending decisions, money drain, and changing conditions. Even with the best of intentions, there were rough spots with the crew, but the care so many people put into our house and the relationships we formed in the process have added additional depth and appreciation to our enjoyment of living in our completed home."

—Susie and Kalen

Specifications	
Exterior Area:	1,463 Square Feet
Interior Area:	1,170 Square Feet
Designer/Architect:	Susie Harrington and Kalen Jones
Contractor/Builder:	Susie Harrington and Kalen Jones
Structural System:	Post and Beam
Exterior Plaster:	Earthen-and-Lime Plaster
Interior Plaster:	Earthen-and-Lime Plaster
Bales:	Oat Straw Laid Flat

One for Themselves

Susie and Kalen have created a legacy of curvaceous strawbale homes in the Moab, Utah, area. This home for themselves is the epitome of their work.

The plan shows offset, straight walls with only curved ends. Walls undulate in height, and the roof is covered with recycled rubber-tire shingles with sensuous curves. The overall impression is one of curves. The terraced landscaping, which leads from the parking area down to the house, is delineated with curved, plastered retaining walls. The curved branches of a juniper post define and support the arched entrance.

Inside, colored earthen floors flow beautifully through the house and combine with the softly colored earthen-plastered wall surfaces and wood ceiling to create a serene and sophisticated atmosphere.

Following the curvilinear theme, the stairs have curved nosings, curved kitchen countertops gracefully surround the open kitchen, and arched openings herald the movement between living spaces.

Susie and Kalen.

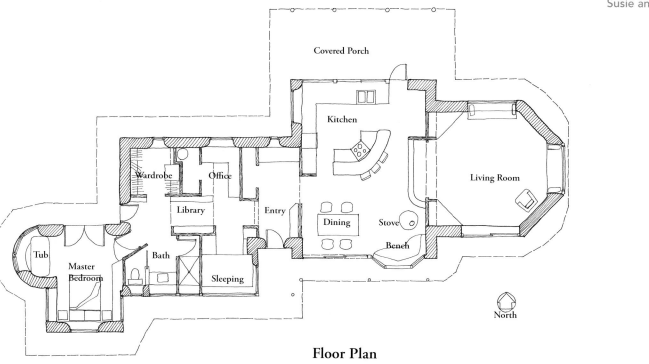

Floor Plan

Kitchen and dining area from the meditation/yoga room flooded with light from the south-facing windows.

The meditation/yoga room is raised two steps above the main living area with a large circular window facing east. Additional north and south windows balance the light in the room.

Small-Town Dream Homes

A juniper post sets off the entrance and helps support the curved roof.

The kitchen with views to the bluff through an open window and screened porch. The open plan allows active participation between cooks and guests.

The deep overhanging roof protects the earthen plaster. The upper roof supports solar panels.

A freestanding, low earthen wall, with stone cap and floral bas-relief features and benches to the sides, will house a future fireplace.

Retirement Residence
for the Future

Brecha-Seidl Residence • Yellow Springs, Ohio

Our Story

"We started thinking about a strawbale house when we were looking for a house to buy as an investment/rental property. Friends who had done strawbale construction before were interested in dividing up their lot to use as building sites and wanted to build more strawbale houses on them. We jumped at the chance and decided to build a house that we can move into once our kids are grown. Our biggest motivation was a desire to own a beautiful, energy-efficient strawbale house, which used solar energy for heat and was built from locally available, natural building materials. We also wanted to raise awareness about strawbale building.

"We financed the project by taking out an equity loan on our current home and then transferred it into a mortgage once the house was finished. Our strawbale-experienced friends Beth and Andy Holyoke were the main builders, and we worked along with them as much as we could.

"We were not able to take a lot of time designing the floor plan because we could only allow for one year of planning and building. In addition, we wanted to keep the cost low, so we went with the simplest shape, a rectangle, but tried to put as many passive solar design features into the house as we could. We designed a roof that would provide both wide overhangs to protect the walls and give shade in the summer but that would also give the proper pitch for solar hot-water panels for radiant floor heat. We could have fretted about the design a lot more and there are a few features that we would do differently like putting the shower on an interior wall instead of next to the strawbale/lime plaster wall—this is already giving us headaches because moisture is getting into the bales—but the house turned out to be beautiful in its simplicity.

"To save on material costs and to give the house some instant character, we bought old doors at a flea market, used recycled barn siding for trim, stained the concrete slab and left it bare, made our own paint and used fun materials like a piece of bowling lane as a countertop.

"Designing and installing the solar system on the roof was a challenge but luckily we knew someone with the know-how and plenty of used solar panels who could help Bob figure out his first solar hot-water system. We learned a lot and hope to be able to help other people get started on solar. This part of Ohio is definitely behind on technology for energy alternatives.

"Since this house is in a very visible spot in the middle of a small town, people stopped by the building site to find out about this weird 'straw house' every day, sometimes making it hard for us to actually get work done. There is a huge amount of interest in this kind of building and the solar technology, and we still get requests to show the house all the time.

Specifications	
Exterior Area:	1,548 Square Feet
Interior Area:	1,353 Square Feet
Designers:	Katharina Seidl, Beth Holyoke, and Bob Brecha
Contractor/Builder:	Beth Holyoke and Andy Holyoke
Structural System:	Post and Beam
Exterior Plaster:	Earthen Plaster
Interior Plaster:	Earthen and Lime Plasters
Bales:	Wheat Straw Laid on Edge with OSB Nailer Plates Every Other Course

"We are recovering from the intensity of the experience of building such a personal house, with all the joy, creativity, labor, anxiety, and exhaustion that goes into it. We know for certain that our two young daughters are glad to have their parents back again! Although we are renting the house to a friend at the moment, we still feel very connected to and proud of our project."

—Bob and Katharina

(left to right) Bob, Katharina, and builder Andy Holyoke.

The dragonflies and floral designs that define the wall color changes illustrate the versatility of expression inherent in natural finishes.

Small-Town Dream Homes

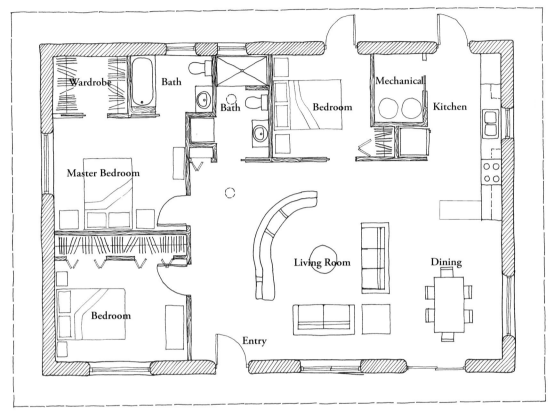

Floor Plan

Simply Solar

This three-bedroom, two-bath, single-story strawbale home is extremely energy efficient with its long axis facing south and ample windows to collect natural light and heat. There are solar collectors on the south-facing roof that provide a large portion of the heating requirements for the house.

The great room includes the kitchen, dining, and living room space. The dining area is particularly light filled with an east window and a south-facing sliding-glass door. One unusual feature is a partial-height wall/bench/fireplace made of clay plaster that separates the bedroom and bathroom entrances from the living space. It also helps to define an entry space.

The floors are dark-stained concrete with radiant heating tubes. Handcrafted wall sculptures depicting butterflies, dragonflies, and tree branches enhance the walls. Changes in color in the wall and the fine detailing reveal the hand of careful craftspeople. Sun tube lighting sources bring natural light into north-facing bathrooms.

The southeast view shows a stone facing on lime-plastered cinder block wall.

Home with Strawbale
Inside Concrete Block

Petersen Residence • Bothwell, Utah

Our Story

"Stan's first encounter with strawbale was at Wasatch Academy in Mt. Pleasant, Utah, where a professor's wife had built a strawbale retreat in her backyard. Stan, a mason and plasterer, was intrigued with the structure and impressed by the straw insulation for heating and cooling as well as sound. He decided then that the next home he would build for his family would be strawbale.

"One year after seeing the strawbale retreat in Mt. Pleasant, we moved to Tremonton, Utah, and Stan planned to build a home. Tremonton is a farming community and had strawbales readily available. So the story begins.

"I drew the floor plan for the home to fit the family lifestyle. A local draftsperson prepared the house plans based on my drawing.

"Being a mason, Stan wanted to lay limestone on the exterior of the home and was stumped about how to affix stone to strawbale, so he decided to build the perimeter shell with cinder block and then stack strawbales on the inside of the home. He could then lay limestone against the exterior of the cinder block.

"The house was built on ground with a high water table so the standard foundation wall was raised and a conventional wood-truss floor system with a crawl space was used. Bales were laid on this wood floor. We also believe this will increase the home's value since loaning institutions in this area would not loan money for a slab on grade.

"Stan anticipates that our next strawbale house will be smaller and in an affordable community. The structure could be a modified strawbale with adobe or compressed earth block.

"The front-porch structural-support timbers, fascia, soffits, and interior support timbers are recycled from the Great Salt Lake train trestle (Trestlewood). There are no latex paints on the exterior or interior; all colors over plaster are natural pigment lime washes.

"The construction loan and long-term mortgage were obtained from a local bank in Tremonton. The building inspector was excited for the first strawbale home to be built in our community.

"Well, now everyone in Tremonton knows about our 'strawbale house' since it is the only one in the area. We are sure there are some who have expected the house to fall down. On the other hand, the local farmers understand the thermal qualities of straw and totally understand the insulation factor.

"Our heating costs are less expensive than with conventional construction, the quietness indoors is a plus, and it's a nice feeling to know we have tread on the environment as little as possible.

"Over the years our home has been opened to friends and strangers curious to see a strawbale home and lime plasters. As a result of building and showing our home, Stan has been given many opportunities in his profession. He travels nine months out of the year to apply natural lime plasters and earthen plasters on strawbale, compressed earth-block, rostra, and adobe homes."

—Stan and Jana

Specifications	
Exterior Area:	2,420 Square Feet
Interior Area:	2,050 Square Feet
Designer/Architect:	Jana Petersen
Contractor/Builder:	Owner
Structural System:	Concrete Block with Interior Strawbale Wrap
Exterior Plaster:	Lime
Interior Plaster:	Lime
Bales:	Wheat Strawbales Attached to Block Wall

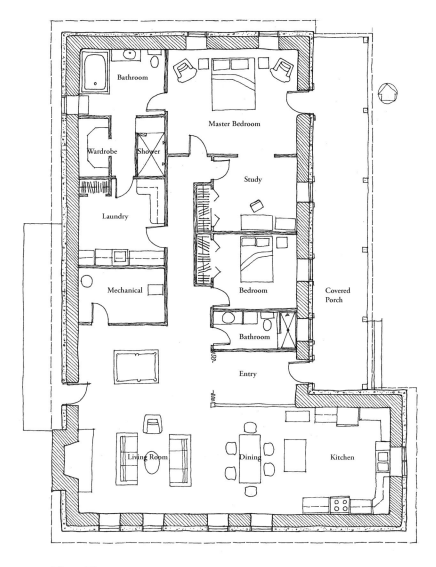

Floor Plan

Unusual Construction Methods

The construction method for this house is one of the most unique we found. A load-bearing shell was used—a 6-inch cinder block wall with strawbales attached to the inner surface. We believe that the block wall would perform better thermally and act as a heat regulator if located on the inside rather than outside of the bales, however.

A generous east-facing porch welcomes visitors and provides shelter from the sun and a place to relax in the afternoon shade.

The house has a crawl space with a suspended first floor due to the high water table. A small furnace supplies heat through ducts in the crawl space. Carpet made from recycled plastic bottles is used throughout. Lime plaster was applied using a variety of techniques and finish effects, creating a museum of different looks with a soft butter yellow in the kitchen and living area, sage green in the bathroom, and a mottled red orange in the entry.

Money-saving ideas abound in the kitchen. Pottery tables were used as kitchen cabinets with exposed shelving for storage of pots and pans, and exposed shelving supports spices. Clay tile enhances the floor.

Stan and Jana.

The deep porch allows for relaxed sitting areas. Windows are accentuated by wide and deep frames, and limestone faces the lower half of the wall. Recycled ceiling wood contrasts with the wall plaster.

A soft sage green finish covers the wall to a height of eight feet. The white finish above increases a sense of space by making the ceiling appear higher. Painted bead board surrounds the tub and base of the independent washstand.

The kitchen features a gas range with a large built-in hood, pottery tables for cabinets, and commercial shelving for the corner storage unit.

Small-Town Dream Homes

With the ground sloping to the east, the house is built with three levels to accommodate the changes in elevation.

Split Levels Stepping
Up a Slope

Carruthers Residence • Santa Fe, New Mexico

My Story

"Having worked in residential construction for a number of years, it had long been my desire to design and build my own home. In the winter of 1999, I had the opportunity to purchase a small parcel of land in the foothills southeast of Santa Fe. A year and a half later, I received a building permit. Four years later, I moved into my house.

"My only building site was near the base of land that slopes eastward, bound by three drainages. I wanted a house big enough to accommodate a couple. I also wanted to feel comfortable building the house myself, incorporating natural and sustainable materials as much as possible and disturbing the site minimally, which was in keeping with the local vernacular.

"There are many natural-building systems to choose from. I chose a light-frame structural system, using strawbales for infill for their higher insulation value, coupled with relative ease of use in terms of labor involved, a major consideration since the labor involved would be my own.

"I placed my wall studs on 18-inch centers to accommodate the width of the bales I would be using. Before beginning any infill work, I completed the roof to protect the bales from any precipitation, a real concern when working alone and when progress is slow.

"The bulk of the infill work went quickly. I used an electric chain saw to notch the bales to envelope the wall studs. The process slowed down considerably, however, when I began making custom bales to fill all the odd spaces created mostly by the door and window openings. Though it took me longer than I anticipated, I was very gratified when I finished that process; the house is very snug.

"Strawbale walls generally take considerably more plaster than other natural walls, but using a clay/straw plaster greatly facilitated that process.

"I was nearly finished with the infill work when my savings were pretty much exhausted. I was fortunate that the parents of friends were able and willing to loan me the money I needed to finish my house. It allowed me to continue working on the house without interruption—a great help. A little over a year later I received my 'CO' (Certificate of Occupancy), at which point I was able to secure a mortgage against the equity in my house for the amount I borrowed.

"I very much enjoyed the process of building my house. Towards the end, after having worked on it steadily for almost two years, I began to tire emotionally. There seemed no end to the finish work, and I was feeling pressure to get moved in. I hired two friends, also builders, who helped for two and a half weeks. They provided a great emotional lift at that point. Friends also helped with the foundation concrete pours,

Specifications	
Exterior Area:	988 Square Feet
Interior Area:	784 Square Feet
Designer/Architect:	Charlie Carruthers and Paula Baker-LaPorte
Contractor/Builder:	Charlie Carruthers
Structural System:	2 x 6-Inch Stud Framing
Exterior Plaster:	Earthen Plaster
Interior Plaster:	Earthen Plaster Applied with Wood Float
Bales:	Barley Straw Laid Vertically and Notched between Studs

window installation, cabinets, doors, plumbing, electrical, and initial plaster coat. It was a wonderful experience.

"There remains finish work to complete: rock veneer around the base of my house, a porch over the main entrance, and numerous interior details.

"Having lived in my house for over a year now, I'm very pleased. There is little I would change. Would I use strawbales again? Most definitely! My advice to future owner-builders is 'keep it small, keep it simple.' That adage applies more than ever as building costs continue to rise. And everything takes longer and costs more than you anticipate. My experience was no exception. Good luck!"

—Charlie

Bathroom window with refined, sharp-edged, angled earthen plaster.

116

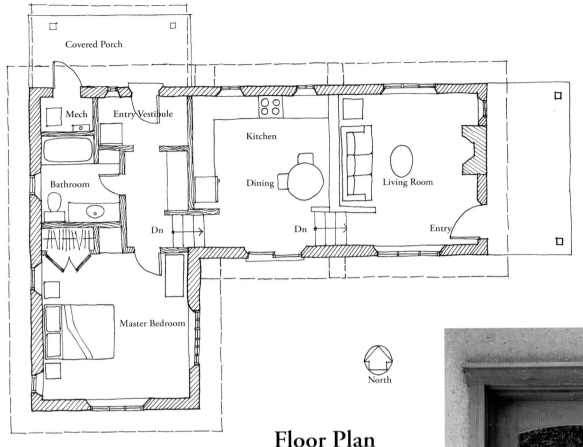

Floor Plan

North

Craftsperson Showpiece

Charlie is an extremely careful and skillful craftsperson whose trade is plastering. His home is a showpiece of beautifully applied earthen plaster inside and out.

The house steps up the sloped lot gracefully with three distinct levels. The bedroom and bath are on the upper level. The kitchen and dining are on the second level and are separated by a partial-height wall that overlooks the living space on the entry level below.

Ample roof overhangs protect the earthen plaster. The front door is custom made. Windows in the house are judiciously placed to balance the natural light.

The custom-made east-entrance wood door is set deep into the strawbale wall.

South-facing bedroom windows bring in welcome heat and light.

Earthen plaster surrounds wood
windows and concrete sills with a
generous drip edge.

Small-Town Dream Homes

The stepped-up wall separates the living room from the stairs to the kitchen.

A walk-out partial basement supports the main-floor kitchen and dining room. Main-level living and bedroom spaces support upper-level studies and studio.

Hillside Three-Story
in a Cohousing Community

Pruitt-Stowell Residence • Port Townsend, Washington

Our Story

"We have a home! We even have homeowner's insurance. This is quite a victory for a strawbale home. We are living here most comfortably since we moved in August 1999, and our home is still standing. Our moisture meter reads '0' at the four stations we test. We are still missing trim (baseboards in the hall, door trim in the laundry room, and so on).

"We are slowly making progress with final paint colors. I have completed a three-tone paint job in the main hallway and a more complex flying-geese wall mural over-painted by glaze in the stairwell. Technically, we are still in an extended temporary occupancy permit due to missing exterior door thresholds (well, the whole front porch!). Still, the house is truly home and quite fabulous!

"Our 2-foot-thick walls keep us snug; the house is quiet even on wild, windy nights. If we want to hear the rain and wind, we have to go upstairs to the 'attic' (the second floor), where the scissor trusses function more like a standard wood-frame home, and the roof windows let in the sound of rain and wind.

"Our small Hearthstone propane heater kept us cozy the first mild winter, and the flickering 'fire' look is nice. It takes a while to bring the temperature up once it is allowed to drop 10 to 15 degrees. With the heat set low at night, the temperature drops more than I expected. To combat this, this year we have a weather seal under the door to the basement and are using our ventilation fans less to reduce heat loss."

—Michael and Sandra

Michael and Sandra.

Specifications	
Exterior Area:	2,563 Square Feet
Interior Area:	2,088 Square Feet
Designer/Architect:	Christopher Stafford
Contractor/Builder:	Owner
Structural System:	Post and Beam
Exterior Plaster:	Cement Stucco
Interior Plaster:	Gypsum
Bales:	Wheat Straw Laid on Edge

The open kitchen serves the dining nook with windows on three sides that overlook the cohousing community beyond.

Pacific Northwest Multilevel Home

Three unique features of this home caught our eye: the accommodation of the plan to the hill slope, the overall height of the building kept lower by use of a half-story upper level, and the fact that this house is the only strawbale building at Rosewind Cohousing. The partial basement level at the base of the slope supports the kitchen and dining nook at the same level as the living room and bedroom. The upper level is above the living/bedroom area, allowing for a cathedral ceiling in the kitchen.

The main living spaces are all conveniently located on the main level. The upper level serves as studio and offices. The walkout basement is a work and storage area.

Finishes are nearing completion on the interior of the house with natural plaster colors contrasting with the wood trusses of the kitchen ceiling. Wood floors are used throughout most of the house, except for linoleum in the kitchen. The countertop is granite, and the island is butcher block with the range at the center to allow for easy conversation while food is being prepared.

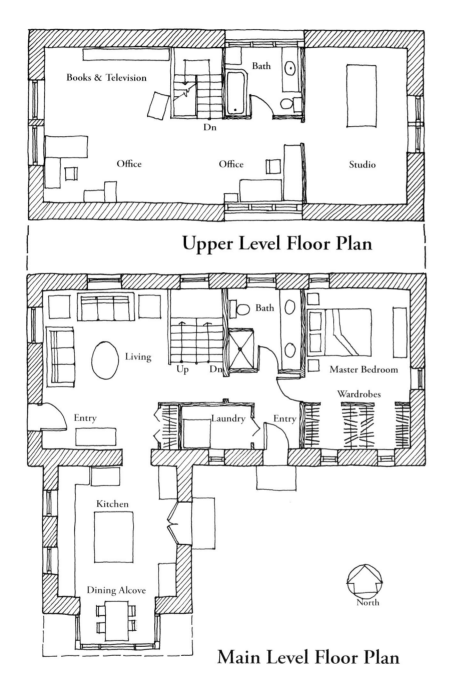

Upper Level Floor Plan

Books & Television

Bath

Dn

Office

Office

Studio

Living

Bath

Up   Dn

Master Bedroom

Wardrobes

Entry

Laundry   Entry

Kitchen

Dining Alcove

North

Main Level Floor Plan

The upper-level sitting area with west window and north skylight.

ADDITIONS AND REMODELS

Two Buildings with Understated Southwest Elegance

Art Studio and Residence • Santa Fe, New Mexico

The Story

"The hacienda-style layout of the art studio and house in Santa Fe, the natural surroundings, and clients who really knew they wanted to be as green as possible made for a great opportunity for a great sustainable project. The original buildings included a strawbale home with a conventional guesthouse with attached garage built in 1997. The remodel project was a wonderful opportunity for Palo Santo Designs, LLC, to push the envelope in green design for a historical Santa Fe territorial-style frame with parapet roofs. Though the original residence was only eight years old, it blended perfectly with the historic adobe homes in the neighborhood. The owners approached Palo Santo Designs for renovating and expanding the compound while maintaining the strawbale construction. Architect Trey Jordan came up with an excellent restructuring of the old garage with straw addition to create a master suite separate from the main house.

"The strawbale system used incorporates 2 x 6-inch studs with strawbale infill, using the bales stacked on end, providing a 14-inch-thick wall. This system was chosen because it would easily integrate with the existing frame structure. The remaining standard 2 x 6-inch construction is insulated with blown-in cellulose insulation.

"The building utilizes two solar-heat collectors mounted on the roof to supply the domestic hot water and radiant in-floor heat. During times of limited sunshine or high demand, the hot-water tank uses a conventional gas-fired heating system to keep hot water and in-floor heat operating normally. In addition to this solar heating, the sun is also utilized to produce electricity that is fed back into the power grid. It is estimated that we are producing about 25 percent of our overall electricity needs with this system.

"The roof has parapets high enough to visually block any of the components of the solar collectors that are mounted there, as required by the Santa Fe Historic Board. From the street one cannot tell that this house is in any way unusual since it fits in perfectly with its historic surroundings. The building has traditional canales to drain rain and snow that melts off the roof into catchment basins underground. Complementing this rain-catchment system is a gray-water irrigation system that functions through one of the catchment basins. Waste water from the bathroom vanities, tub, and steam shower is piped to a catchment basin and utilized for landscape irrigation. Toilet water is not linked to this system and goes directly to the city sewer.

"The interior of the house is beautifully finished using nontoxic, natural, and green products. The floor and the overhead beams of the bedroom are recycled antique wood salvaged from demolition projects. The built-in wood shelving is made of fire-killed Douglas fir from the Pecos Forest fire nearby. The vanity top, matching vanity chest of drawers, and walk-in closet shelving are constructed with a combination of formaldehyde-free MDF and recycled antique wood. The walls are plastered with all-natural clay plaster from American Clay, previously known as Clayote. And the garage interior is painted with nontoxic paint from Bioshield.

The east-facing portal entry to the studio is defined by a low white-painted wood railing that provides a semiprivate sitting space.

Specifications		
	Studio	**Master Studio**
Exterior Area:	3,618 Square Feet	1,008 Square Feet
Interior Area:	3,000 Square Feet	806 Square Feet
Designer/Architect:	Steve Robinson, Trey Jordan, and Palo Santo Designs	
Contractor/Builder:	Living Structures and Palo Santo Designs	
Structural System:	Load Bearing and Post and Beam	
Exterior Plaster:	Cement Plaster Applied with Steel Trowels	
Interior Plaster:	Clay	
Bales:	Wheat Straw Stacked on End between Studs	

"After completion of the master suite, Palo Santo Designs designed an expansion and remodel of the original main house. We tore out a bathroom and all partition walls to create an art studio and gallery space for the owners to display their work. A malfunctioning fountain and enclosed courtyard were gutted and incorporated into a new kitchen/dining/living room expansion, which included an adobe fireplace by Charlie Carruthers and exquisite interior woodwork by the crew of PSD, led by master craftsman Robert Godreau. Interior walls were plastered with clay plasters, and all wood finishes are from Bioshield. The addition was constructed with modified post and beam and strawbale infill to match the existing strawbale construction. The super-insulated roof with blown-in cellulose and 5 inches of spray-applied urethane roofing gives "cozy" a new meaning. This place is tight, clean, and elegantly earthy. It brings strawbale construction into high-end Santa Fe. Many thanks to the artistically inspired and generous owners who trusted us to do our magic the best way we knew how.

"This project is an excellent example of how environmentally sound and innovative green-building systems can and should be incorporated into contemporary, aesthetically pleasing, and culturally appropriate designs. Green construction can be easily achieved within the context of mainstream and high-end custom construction."

—Mark Giorgetti, Palo Santo Designs

Sophisticated Santa Fe Remodel and Addition

We visited the original building site while it was under construction in 1998. It was a residence and a garage. The new owners of the buildings have converted the garage into a master suite with living, sleeping, and bathing quarters, while retaining food preparation and dining in the original building. There has been an addition to the original building as well as remodeling.

The subtle welcoming of light into the building through skylights and appropriately placed windows creates a beautiful ambiance in hallways, bathroom, and entry. Electric light complements the natural light. Brick pavers in the entry and wood floors throughout the remainder of the house combine with the soft coloring of the natural plastered walls for a warm, inviting feeling. Mark Giorgetti found some old wood columns, which are used to support the original structure, that provide strong visual elements in the living and kitchen areas. Wood louvered doors cover an entertainment center. Some doors existed and some were replicated to match the original wood louvered doors. New bookshelves with cabinet storage below were added to the living area.

Lace curtains that cover French doors on two opposing walls in the master suite allow in muted light. A custom two-sided bookshelf/partition separates the sleeping area from the living and television space.

We were particularly impressed with the camaraderie of the skilled craftsmen and other workers on the site. They made it a point to express to us their appreciation for the positive energy involved in working together with the homeowners in creating beauty and elegance in a sustainable way.

The library wall and fireplace separate the bedroom from the living space in the master suite.

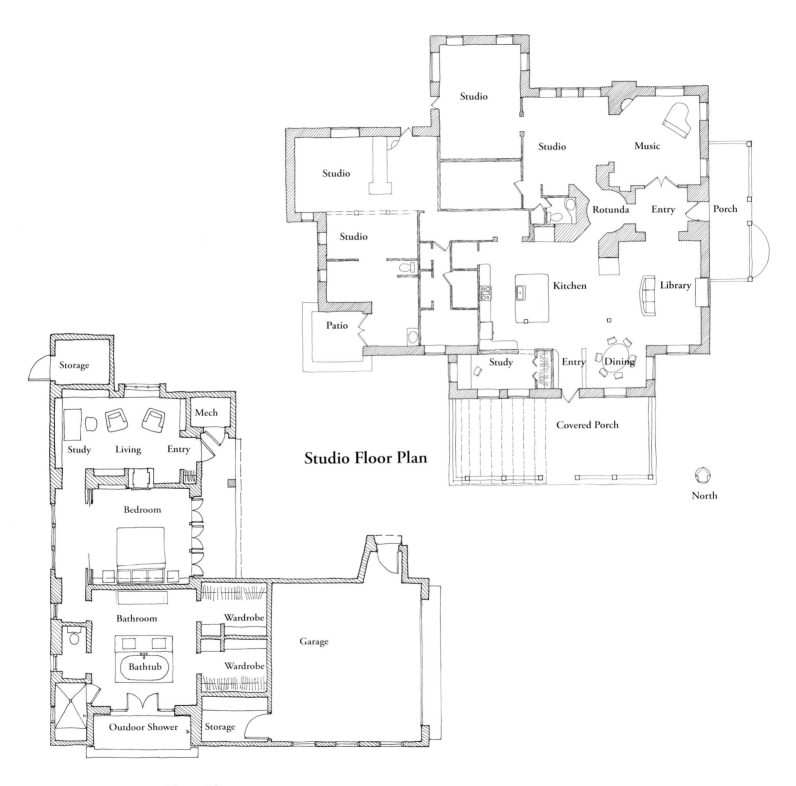

Studio

Studio   Music

Studio

Rotunda   Entry   Porch

Studio

Kitchen   Library

Patio

Study   Entry   Dining

Studio Floor Plan

Covered Porch

North

Storage

Mech

Study   Living   Entry

Bedroom

Bathroom   Wardrobe

Garage

Bathtub   Wardrobe

Outdoor Shower   Storage

Living Quarters Floor Plan

Tall windows and soft, warm hues covering thick strawbale walls articulate the library and dining spaces.

Additions and Remodels

Built-in wood grilles and cabinets articulate the library space. The rotunda is on the left and the east entry is on the right.

The rotunda space has a skylight to bring light into the interior circulation node.

The bedroom has lace-curtain-covered French doors on both sides of the room, which allow soft, diffused light.

Additions and Remodels

The bathroom is a soft green. The tub and sinks are at the center, and the shower and toilet are in enclosed spaces beyond.

Garage Conversion
to a Wellness Center

Indigo Wellness Center • Cochranton, Pennsylvania

Our Story

"The Indigo Center was originally conceived to be a healing and retreat center. We had felt the need to provide a space with an atmosphere of peace and harmony in order to host workshops, ceremonies, lectures, art, music, various healing modalities, and retreats. Since we wanted the space to provide a feeling of harmony, we realized that the materials we used had to be acquired and applied with this same feeling. Using natural materials was the only option that made sense.

"It's difficult to describe the feeling you get inside a straw-insulated, earthen-plastered space; it's almost as if you're being embraced by the earth. While it felt wonderful collecting and using these materials, it didn't feel so nice going to the lumberyard to buy wood supplies. We both really enjoy walking in the woods, being surrounded by mature trees and the life they harbor. Living in a wooded area of western Pennsylvania, we see a lot of timbering activity around us, and even 'sustainable harvests' can be quite disruptive. We began to realize that if we held off on a trip to the building-supply store, what we needed would soon show up on the side of the road, in someone's trash heap, or in a burn pile, and always with good timing as long as we kept our eyes open. Interestingly, since we shifted to this way of thinking, we haven't had to buy a single piece of commercial lumber. We've been able to salvage enough lumber for framing, doors, windows, trim, and even cabinets simply by putting the word out and staying aware.

"As we delved deeper into the source of the materials we were using, we started to feel that it wasn't enough that they be sustainably produced; they had to be harmoniously produced as well. Was it possible to not disturb any lives or any ecosystems in the process? We've found that by using salvaged materials, not only does that goal seem possible, but there's a mushroom effect. You wind up helping to reduce the landfill burden on the earth and the pollution levels in the air. Another benefit that we didn't expect is that we've been able to provide employment to friends and neighbors in need since handling natural and salvaged materials is labor intensive. Instead of giving the money to mega industry, we've been able to help support individuals in the community.

"The Indigo Center's purpose has expanded and evolved as a result of the construction process. We've become aware of such a need to help develop and educate others about ways to live more harmoniously on the earth. As more and more people are becoming aware of our place on the planet and seeking harmonious alternatives to conventional building practices, our educational efforts have become a huge part of our efforts. We now offer education on natural food growing and collecting and living in harmony with animal life as well. We see a community of people forming around all of these activities. The Indigo Center has become a center for harmonious living."

—Mary and Gene

Lime and earthen-plaster finishes
in upper-level library.

Specifications	
Exterior Area:	1,960 Square Feet
Interior Area:	1,560 Square Feet
Designer/Architect:	Gene Leone
Contractor/Builder:	Gene Leone
Structural System:	Post and Beam
Exterior Plaster:	Earthen-and-Lime Plaster
Interior Plaster:	Earthen-and-Lime Plaster
Bales:	Two-String Bales on Edge

The ground-level entrance to a group meeting room has a built-in bench, lime-finished walls, and an earthen floor.

A deep window brings soft light into a meeting room.

Handcrafted Addition

Mary and Gene have been building their rural health and healing center to accommodate long-term guests and provide individual and group therapy for several years. The original wood-sided house is contrasted with a new lime-plastered two-story strawbale addition. Group meeting rooms are on the first floor, heated by a custom-built masonry heater. The second floor includes a meeting room, library, kitchen, and massage rooms.

We were impressed with the handcrafted quality of the work, earthen floors, natural vegetation bas-reliefs sculpted onto the walls, lime on portions of the walls separated by an ochre color band from the earthen plasters, and the wood lath ceilings. A work in progress, the building demonstrates the use of strawbales beyond the single-family dwelling.

Upper-level rooms have earthen-paint finishes and oil-finished earthen floors.

Gene and Mary.

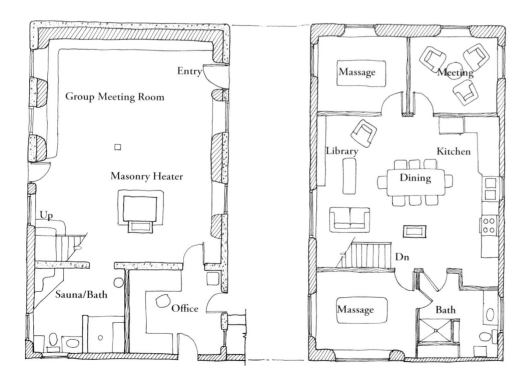

Ground Level Floor Plan

Entry

Group Meeting Room

Masonry Heater

Up

Sauna/Bath

Office

North

Upper Level Floor Plan

Massage

Meeting

Library

Kitchen

Dining

Dn

Massage

Bath

A custom-built masonry heater provides heat for the new addition as well as hot water for domestic use. The exposed timber frame structure supports the second level above.

The southeast view in the fall of 2000. Freshly white-washed lime walls, a barrel vaulted roof, and blue shutters reflect local Greek building traditions.

Ecological Villa
on the Beach

Ecological Villa • Apolakia, Rhodes, Greece

The Story

"Italians Susanna Fioretti and her partner, Marco, built their future retirement house in Glikorizo (meaning 'sweet root,' or licorice that grows naturally in the surrounding fields) on the Island of Rhodes in the Aegean Sea. They had adjacent property on the beach they wanted to use for the benefit of needy children, particularly orphans of war-torn countries. The original idea was to 'build a house, adopt a few children, and live in the house like a wide family.'

"Susanna advertised on the Internet to find someone interested in designing and building a sustainable building on her property. Chris Stafford, an American architect, was selected to assist her in the design of the building, and American Gene Leone, with a background in natural building in the United States, Mexico, and France, was selected to build it.

"The design is a set of five parallel and adjacent one-story rectangular units, approximately 300 square feet each, offset from one another by half of their length. Except for the vaulted unit, the structure was designed to be consistent with the indigenous Greek residential architecture. The strawbale walls are load bearing and have wood rafters supporting a local reed ceiling with 6-inch straw clay for insulation and a lime-plaster roof coating. All roofs are gently sloped 1/4 inch per foot and drain to wide scuppers.

"Two of the five modules were begun in April 1999 and virtually finished in October of that year. The remaining three modules were started in April 2000 and brought close to finish in October and early November of 2000.

"The photo on the opposite page shows how the house looked the morning we left Greece, November 5, 2000, after two weeks of intense work by approximately a dozen people."

—Wayne Bingham

Susanna.

Specifications	
Exterior Area:	1,592 Square Feet
Interior Area:	1,170 Square Feet
Designer/Architect:	Christopher Stafford
Contractor/Builder:	Gene Leone and Volunteers from around the World
Structural System:	Load Bearing
Exterior Plaster:	Lime Plaster over Earthen Base Coats Applied by Hand and Trowel
Interior Plaster:	Lime Plaster over Earthen Base Coats Applied by Hand and Trowel
Bales:	Wheat Two-String Laid Flat with Bamboo External Pins

Glikorizo Beach Home for Children

The design and finishes of Susanna's house reflect indigenous Greek architectural style. The white lime finish reflects the brilliant Mediterranean light. Simple and forthright like Greek island buildings, the five wings are modulated to break down the scale of the space requirements to match its cultural context.

Small windows were selected to reduce the glare of the sun yet provide enough light. Blue-painted shutters, doors, and window moldings reflect the blue of the Aegean Sea. The interiors have a handmade feel with built-in sleeping accommodations and clothes-storage areas.

Heavy rains caused water damage to the building in 2003. Susanna considered demolishing the building and replacing it with concrete block. However, a solution to keep water away from the bale walls was selected. The subsequent retrofitting included a wraparound porch and a waterproof roof membrane. Remediation appears to have corrected the problems.

The southwest view after 2004 retrofit.

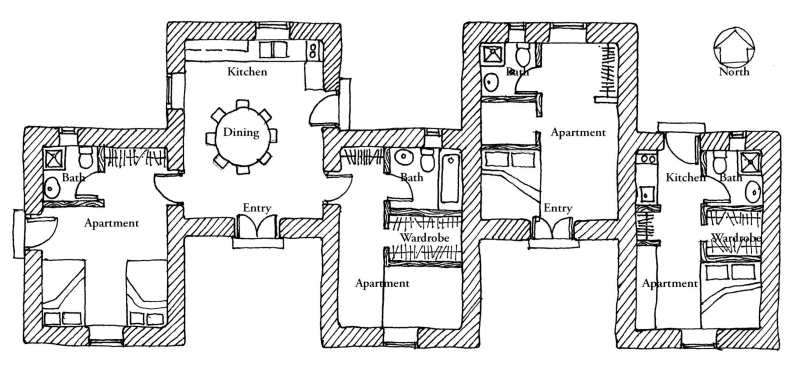

Floor Plan

The southeast view in 2004 after the retrofit, which includes a wraparound porch and new roof membrane for weather protection.

The lime-plastered bathroom features beach-tumbled marble stone trim.

Traditional Greek sleeping platform and loft. The bathroom and entry are beyond. The exposed wood rafters support the carrizo (reed) ceiling and the earthen and lime-plastered roof.

The kitchen and dining space carry the spare Mediterranean feel into the interior.

Additions and Remodels

COTTAGES AND STUDIOS

Living roof, mottled walls, and deep windows distinguish this guesthouse.

French Country Guesthouse

Gardner Guest Cottage • Lincoln, Nebraska

Our Story

"When we built our Tudor-style house on a three-acre tract in 1987, we did not envision building a strawbale guesthouse on the property. Never having lived on acreage before, 'low maintenance' was our mantra when it came time to plan our landscaping. It didn't take us long, however, to get bitten by the gardening bug. By the second spring we were planting and transplanting trees and shrubs as quickly as our budget would allow. We plotted out a vegetable garden and small flowerbeds. By 1992, we had added a conservatory/greenhouse to the house and encompassed within the garden were a pond, swimming pool, and tennis court.

"If you have ever owned a pool, you know how much foot traffic you get running in and out of the house to use the bathroom when guests are over. After a few years of worrying about wet feet and soggy carpets, we decided it was time to build a separate pool house. Walt came up with the idea of building a sod house because he thought it would be indigenous to Nebraska. After consulting with Carl Schreiner, a good friend who also constructed our deck and conservatory, we settled on strawbale construction since he said strawbale was actually more indigenous to the state of Nebraska than sod.

"The plan was to build a small pool house, no more than 800 square feet, which could double as a guesthouse. The project became complicated because of building codes in the county in which we resided for two reasons: One, strawbale construction had not been addressed in the modern era, and there were concerns about the fire hazard. Two, the roof was to be planted with perennials and there were concerns about the weight of the roof. After many months and additional concrete footings and support structures for the roof, our strawbale 'cottage' came to fruition.

"We did not help stack and pin the bales but we helped spray on and trowel the stucco inside and out. We also did all the finishing work inside (including the electrical and plumbing) as well as put the soil on the roof and did the planting. Our strawbale cottage was built to look like an antique French cottage, and we furnished it with old auction finds. The roof is a delight with something blooming most times of the year. Even in winter the different textures provide warmth and interest. Someone once said the roof looks like a patchwork quilt."

—Sue and Walter

Traditional European door knocker with metal hinge and details highlight the heavy wood entrance door.

Specifications	
Exterior Area:	441 Square Feet
Interior Area:	324 Square Feet
Designer/Architect:	Rod Laucomer
Contractor/Builder	Carl Schreiner
Structural System:	Post and Beam
Exterior Plaster:	Cement Stucco
Interior Plaster:	Gypsum

Living area and entry. Wood posts are left flush with the white-plastered walls and contrast with the wood ceiling.

White plaster walls between exposed, rough-finished wood timber frame recall older European construction. Furnishings were selected to enhance the country farmhouse feeling.

Exposed timber framing supports the heavy weight of the living roof. The white-walled European cottage–style kitchen space has an antique hutch. The bathroom beyond, with its own interior roof, appears to be a separate building within the larger room.

Cottages and Studios

Antique French Country with Living Roof

The Gardner guest cottage gives one the impression that it was built in rural France many years ago and helicopter lifted and set in the suburban backyard garden. You approach the building on brick pavers that also could be centuries old. The roof structure supporting the living roof overhangs the rusticated plaster walls and also appears as if it has been here for centuries.

Inside, the French country feeling is continued with an all-white kitchen hutch, tables, wash basins, and chairs.

The white-painted wood bathroom looks like a small building inside the cottage, complete with an interior roof that slopes to the kitchen and dining area. It adds an attractive dimension to the interior of the building.

The supporting posts and roof structure are made of robust, heavy timber frame needed to support the living roof.

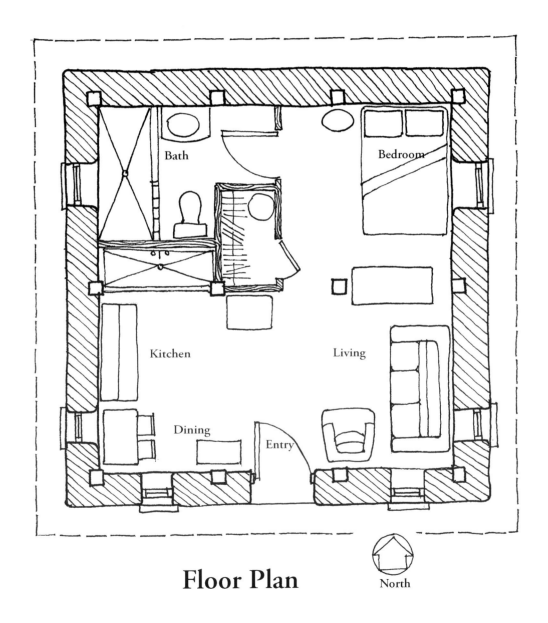

Floor Plan

North

Exterior posts allow free articulation of hand-sculpted strawbale walls and window detail.

Artistic
Garden Studio

Garrette Studio • Lawrence, Kansas

Our Story

"From what we had seen of strawbale buildings in books and magazines, we liked the hand-sculpted, organic look that could be achieved with layers of plaster. The use of natural materials appealed to us as well. We don't like to use chemical-based products in our everyday lives (e.g., household cleaners, soaps, nonorganic food), so the thought of building without chemicals made a lot of sense. It felt like an earth-friendly option, without the off-gassing of conventional construction materials. We used local products and produced little waste. Any straw that was left over was used as mulch in the garden. A highly insulated building also seemed practical for the cold Kansas winters and hot, humid summers.

"Basically we needed studio space for our art. Our home is less than 800 square feet, and with two small children, it was impossible to have projects going in the house. Victoria had been reading *Natural Home Magazine* for a few years and was taken with the idea of natural building. I was excited about it when I saw some clippings of homes featured in the magazine. The next thing we knew we were drawing up plans and applying for a building permit. It made sense to us to build something that we felt good about as far as energy efficiency and organic materials.

"We thought we would have a lot more time to work on it, but it turned out to be me working on it mostly on my own, part-time, for about two years. We had help from friends with the foundation, roof, bale stacking, and plastering work. This was great because it is not a style of building that many people are familiar with but most find very intriguing and accessible. We are very excited to have the last coat of beeswax drying on the earthen floor—we'll be able to start using the space soon.

"From this studio we have learned how to build a home that we love to be in and outside of. The right clay for the plaster is very important. Do tests with the plaster, floor, and paint materials, and then do more to become more familiar with the working properties of the material. Network to find people who are interested in helping; they are out there. The straighter and tighter the bales, the less plasterwork required. This is very important to consider if someone wants to do most of the work themselves since mixing plaster of any type takes time and lots of energy. Our 2 x 4 stick-frame house feels like a cardboard box in comparison to the studio!

"We love the window detail, curves, and swirls in the plaster and decorative natural paints; the uneven, sculptural quality of the walls; and the relief sculptures incorporated into the final coats of plaster. We took advantage of transition points in the final coats of plaster to add sculptural curves. People seeing the studio for the first time are really delighted by its playful qualities. There are some things, however, that we would do differently. We would wood frame a larger area for utilities to be mounted. We would do the earthen floor absolutely last so it would be

Victoria, Scott, and family.

Specifications	
Exterior Area:	550 Square Feet
Interior Area:	400 Square Feet
Designer/Architect:	Victoria and Scott Garrett
Contractor/Builder:	Victoria and Scott Garrett
Structural System:	External Post and Beam
Exterior Plaster:	Earthen Plaster with Lime Trim Applied by Hand and Trowel
Interior Plaster:	Earthen Plaster Applied by Hand and Trowel
Bales:	Two-String Wire Wheat Bales on Edge with External Wood and Bamboo Pinning

White lime surrounds some windows while different colors of clay paint surround others.

A Very Personal Expression

Scott and Victoria created—with a great deal of effort, determination, and skill—a delightful, very personal art studio in their small, urban backyard.

The roof is supported by posts that are external to the wall surface, creating an overhang that protects the plaster from the weather. The windows and door vary in size and shape based on their source. They are integrated into the walls in pleasing, playful ways. The colorful, curving, and artful surfaces are a delight for the eye. The studio feels and looks handmade. It is a place kids of all ages enjoy playing in and around.

left undisturbed to dry. We would find a source for clay first and have it delivered. Testing—more, more, and more. We would install 2-inch material where the plaster meets the ceiling and soffit to avoid cracking at the joint due to flex.

"Our studio is a symbol of perseverance. It is a testament to the ability to do what you put your mind to. This structure is a product of our determination, creativity, and faith in our skills. We set a goal—we wanted to build a studio in our backyard—and then took the leap into the unknown. There were many changes along the way and concessions to be made, but we have ended up with a finished product that we love, that feels great to be in, and that we are proud of. Hopefully the attention it has received will inspire others."

—Scott and Victoria

Reed mat and bamboo adorn the ceiling and post.

Playful use of color on the interior of the studio combines with the artistic design of the windows and built-in shelves.

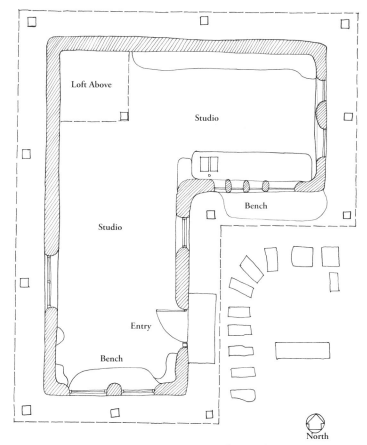

Loft Above

Studio

Bench

Studio

Entry

Bench

North

Floor Plan

COMMUNITY BUILDINGS

The loft is supported by twice-lightning-struck timber. The masonry heater below the loft provides radiant heat to the large room.

Lofty Strawbale-Wrapped Timber Frame

The Dojo • Taos, New Mexico

Our Story

"One of the architectural jewels hidden at the foot of the Sangre de Cristo Mountains in Taos, New Mexico, is called the Dojo. *Dojo* is a Japanese Shinto term referring to a temple setting where the perfection of one's art and the cultivation of one's spirit is practiced. This 1700-square-foot martial arts dojo and performance studio serves as an inspiring, noncommercial venue for friends and family. Yoga, dance, performance, celebrations, ceremonies, as well as educational presentations are but a few of the events that take place regularly at the Dojo.

"The design is dictated by the trees and is a collaboration of John Murray, master chainsaw artist; Ken Anderson and Pam Freund of Edge Architecture; Bob Bassarra, builder/designer; and myself, Elliot Haas, owner. The design maximizes energy efficiency while utilizing natural, renewable, and recycled materials whenever possible. All timbers were cut and joined freehand by John Murray with his chainsaw and his deep respect and love of trees, which are beautifully exemplified in the forest-like ambiance of the interior of the structure.

"The timbers were harvested from the aftermath of the May 5, 1996, type-one Lama Mountain forest fire north of Taos, New Mexico. The trees were left standing after the fire, but they were dead, completely burned on the outside, but structurally sound and even still running sap after the fast-moving fire. In the Dojo, all of the timber frame and nearly all of the trim work are crafted from this reclaimed lumber, including the wood floor in the loft, countertops, and much of the furniture.

"Locally harvested barley-strawbale-infill walls provide an insulation value of R-45. South-facing adobe walls serve as efficient mass solar collectors. The walls are plastered on the exterior with cement stucco and on the interior with natural micaceous adobe plaster with a gypsum plaster base.

"The floor of the 800-square-foot main hall is bamboo tongue and groove. The roofing material is a slate-look shingle made from recycled rubber and plastic. The solar greenhouse area includes a koi pond with a carved wood bridge and planters that recycle gray water. The building is heated primarily with solar gain, and the heat is stored in the adobe mass walls of the greenhouse. Backup heat is provided by a highly efficient masonry stove.

The rewards of this structure are ongoing and self-evident. By honoring and emulating nature in form, function, and resource, aesthetics transcend mere appearance. The Dojo has a spirit of its own. To enter the building is to truly enter into the spirit of wonder and reverence. The timbers and crafted wood resonate with their history of life, fire, tragedy, and resurrection."

—Elliot and Kasey

Specifications	
Exterior Area:	1,662 Square Feet
Interior Area:	1,380 Square Feet
Designer/Architect:	Ken Anderson and Pam Freund
Contractor/Builder:	John Murray, Bob Bassarra, and Elliott Haas
Structural System:	Exposed Post and Beam Wrapped with Strawbales
Exterior Plaster:	Cement Plaster Applied by Hand
Interior Plaster:	Gypsum and Earthen Plaster Applied by Hand; Clay Paint by Carole Crews
Bales:	Barley Bales Laid Flat with Rebar Internal Pins

Reclaimed Timber Masterpiece

Strawbale walls with a beautiful clay paint by Carole Crews wrap around the reclaimed timber frame by John Murray. John's unique way of building amazed us. He used fire-killed wood from nearby forest fires. Bark is removed, but the evidence of the fire remains and is expressed. The joints are all made using a chainsaw. We couldn't believe how the joints could be cut with a chainsaw until he took us to the mill and showed us his process. One post was hit by lightning twice and is featured as the center post supporting the loft.

Wood floors and the glow of the mica-filled clay paint on the walls filled with natural light from windows and the clerestory above, along with rugs, wall hangings, and sculpture, make the place lofty, warm, and serene. John Murray made all of the benches that surround the room

A clay-plastered masonry heater provides even heat that radiates from below the loft, warming the entire space. The Dojo is privately owned and is used primarily for martial arts instruction but is also used for weddings, massage therapy, and community activities.

The south view of the Dojo, with a clerestory roof and wind sculpture. This building was built on reclaimed wetlands.

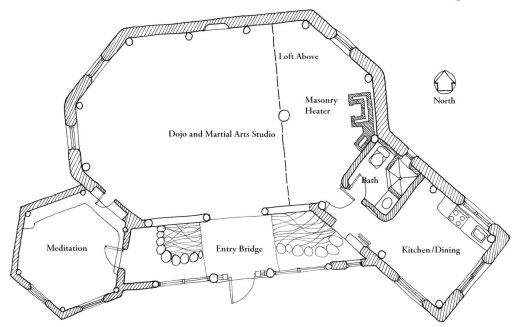

Floor Plan

The entrance leads across a wood-crafted bridge over the ponds filled with water vegetation.

The exposed timber frame with soft-colored walls highlight the lofty central room of the Dojo. The timber frame was crafted using fire-killed standing timber from a nearby forest fire.

157

An overall view from the south shows the meeting rooms on the left and offices on the right.

Sandhill Crane–Shaped Strawbale Bird Watch

Iain Nicholson Audubon Center at Rowe Sanctuary • Gibbon, Nebraska

Their Story

"The Iain Nicholson Audubon Center at the Rowe Sanctuary on the beautiful Platte River was built using strawbales following a pioneer tradition in the Nebraska area from the late 1800s. The straw was harvested and purchased from a local farmer and provides an insulative value of R40 to R50. At the time it was built, it was one of the largest strawbale buildings in Nebraska, using over 760 strawbales in its walls. The straw is held in place with long bamboo spikes and then plastered with sprayed cement stucco, which our builder, Carl Schreiner, said was the hardest and most labor-intensive part of the job.

"The building also has taken advantage of recycled, salvaged, and green materials wherever possible. Cedar tree trunks were gathered from nearby Martins Reach State Wildlife Management Area and the 3 x 14-inch beams were taken from an old warehouse in eastern Nebraska to carry the load of the ceiling in the great room. Ponderosa pine culled from a local forest was used for the ceiling.

"The center also uses a closed-loop geothermal heating-and-cooling system, high-efficiency windows and skylights, as well as shredded, old blue jeans for insulation in the non-bale walls. Cedar siding was made from logs pulled out of the Niobrara River Valley by the Nature Conservancy staff and cut at a local mill. We also used sustainably harvested wood and bought locally whenever possible.

"The use of strawbales and other natural materials gives people a much greater appreciation of natural forms and is more in touch with our natural environment. Thousands of visitors come to the Rowe Sanctuary each year to view the birds and marvel at our facility and how good it feels."

The Rowe Sanctuary

Rowe Bird Sanctuary is another example of a building outside the single-family dwelling prototype that utilizes the benefits of strawbale technology.

Rowe Bird Sanctuary is built on the edge of the Platte River where sandhill cranes spend a portion of the year during their migration. The shape of the building resembles the bird in flight with outstretched wings and pointed bill raised to the sky.

Strawbales are used in the classroom wing to the west and the office wing to the east. A long observation hall extends along the west wing and is constructed of structural insulated panels to keep wall thickness to a minimum, allowing the observers close access to the glass wall. The strawbale walls enclose the meeting rooms behind the observation hall.

Visitors arrive at the central entrance by walking under a wood-trellised porch supported with local wood posts. The floors are stained concrete. An overhead air-distribution system is used to heat and cool the building. This quiet place to observe one of nature's beautiful birds is carefully sited on the land next to the river.

Specifications	
Exterior Area:	5,700 Square Feet
Interior Area:	4,730 Square Feet
Designer/Architect:	Carl Schreiner
Contractor/Builder:	Schreiner Construction
Structural System:	Post and Beam
Exterior Plaster:	Cement over Chicken Wire and Metal Lath
Interior Plaster:	Cement over Chicken Wire and Metal Lath
Bales:	Two-String Wire, Wheat Straw Laid Flat

The soaring roof of the central observation room and the building wings symbolize the sandhill crane in flight.

IAIN
NICOLSON
Audubon
CENTER

at Rowe Sanctuary
Gibbon, Nebraska

Your portal to
nature along Nebraska's
Platte River

Visitor's brochure of the Rowe Sanctuary showing the sandhill cranes that draw observers to the Audubon Center.

Community Buildings

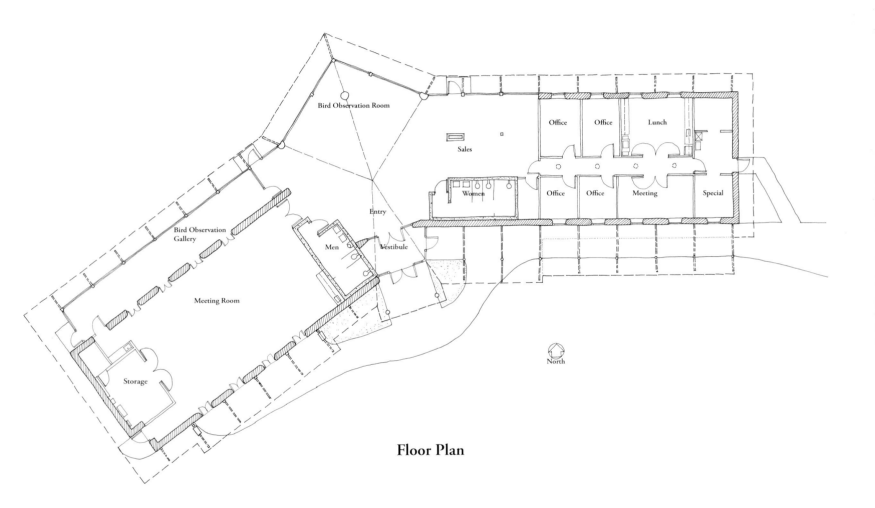

Bird Observation Room

Sales

Office   Office   Lunch

Entry

Bird Observation
Gallery

Men   Women   Office   Office   Meeting   Special

Vestibule

Meeting Room

North

Storage

Floor Plan

The entry walkway is covered
by a wood trellis supported
by native wood posts.

162

The west observation hall, looking out toward the Platte River.

The Tree House, designed by Sun Ray Kelley, is a strawbale, adobe, and light clay/straw hybrid residence with a solarium on the south side and clerestory windows to the two dwelling units. The timber frame structure is external to the enclosure.

The Lama Foundation
Spiritual Community

Lama Foundation • Lama, New Mexico

A Continuing Exploration
of Natural Building

The Lama Foundation is a spiritual community on the side of a mountain north of Taos, New Mexico, that has risen again out of the ashes of a forest fire to embrace natural-building methods and materials with great gusto. Catherine Wanek has organized "Build Here Now," a natural-building convergence that meets yearly, and the Lama Foundation campus has benefited from the contributions of pioneers in the field coming to lead workshops and provide inspiration and direction.

We present here not a single building, but a collage of many of the building types represented there: strawbale, clay/straw, adobe, and timber frame buildings. They vary in character and expression, exploring the full spectrum of owner-built natural building. We found gable roofs, arches, domes, shed dormers, and timber frame systems. The Lama Foundation is a work in progress—many projects have been started that require finishing—but hopefully with careful attention will mature into a more significant place as buildings are completed and the trees restore themselves on the mountainside.

This utility building houses the solar battery bank and is constructed of adobe with earthen plaster. The building is heated by passive solar glazing. The round ferro-cement cistern on the left holds water from the rainwater collection system.

West view of the Tree House with a separate earthen-plastered outhouse.

This load-bearing strawbale residence is located a few hundred feet east of the main community building.

The north side of the Tree House shows the exposed timber frame structure, which uses locally harvested trees from the fire.

Strawbales form the curved vault and gable ends of this residence.

Robert and Paula Baker-Laporte designed this "Econest" residence. It is a timber frame structure that is wrapped with light clay/straw walls.

The *portal* is an outdoor dining facility with superb western views of the Taos plateau. The timber frame structure was built in a workshop setting with Mark Georgetti as designer and workshop leader.

The Dome is an adobe-walled structure with a wooden geodesic domed roof. Note the skylights that admit natural light into the center of the space.

The workshop is passively heated by south-facing windows. The massive timber frame structure is internal, and the exterior walls are earthen-plastered strawbale and light clay/straw.

The greenhouse was designed with deep-colored lime plaster, polycarbonate roof glazing, and clear south-facing glass to fit with the character of the historic central-city neighborhood.

Natural Passive Solar Greenhouse

Wasatch Community Gardens • Salt Lake City, Utah

Our Story

"Wasatch Community Gardens has provided garden plots for local residents and has educated children about organic gardening practices for fifteen years, all without the support facilities of a greenhouse or restroom.

"The nonprofit organization conducted a capital campaign, obtained the building permit after local historic district committee review and approval, and organized workshops to build the strawbale greenhouse and a separate timber framing workshop to build the free-standing learning shelter north of the building.

"On October 1, 2004, the excavation began. On October 31, the building was up and the timber frame was assembled in two hours. There was additional work on the interior, including brick pavers and plaster, but the structure was essentially up and weathered in one month.

"The south-facing greenhouse is glazed with double-hung windows and fixed, double-cell polycarbonate on the roof. The operable windows allow nighttime cooling of the space and venting during the heat of the day. There are also thermostatically operated vents at the top of each gable end to exhaust hot air. There is a full-height concrete-block wall filled with grout at the center of the building that carries the roof load and serves as thermal mass to absorb heat gained from the greenhouse and moderate the indoor temperature.

"A restroom and utility room are located on the north of the building and are heated passively from the central-block thermal mass. All water is conducted away from the building with gutters and downspouts.

"There was tremendous public support and interest during the construction process. Volunteers came from out of thin air. There was a festive and energetic community involvement. We are proud of our new facility."

—Wasatch Community Gardens

Artist's rendering of the greenhouse from the brochure used for fundraising. The brochure was sent to potential donors and civic organizations during the design and building process.

Specifications	
Exterior Area:	650 Square Feet
Interior Area:	506 Square Feet
Architect:	Wayne J. Bingham
Contractor/Builder:	A & G Construction Plus;
	Workshop Participants and Volunteers
Structural System:	Concrete Block Piers at Corners, Post and Beam
Exterior Plaster:	Lime over Earthen Applied by Hand and Trowel
Interior Plaster:	Lime over Earthen Applied by Hand and Trowel
Bales:	Wheat Two-String Bales Laid Flat with
	External Bamboo Pinning

A central supporting concrete-block wall and corner piers with strawbale infill.

Earthen-plaster base coat and rough framing prior to final finishes.

Timber frame profiled against a dark red lime-plastered wall.

Urban Garden Greenhouse

Wasatch Community Gardens greenhouse is an example of how the efforts of an involved board and staff, some professional assistance, and the energy of workshop participants and volunteers can be organized to meet a community need.

There is no supplemental heat in the building so it depends on the sun for its heat source. Heat gain through south-facing glazing is absorbed by the concrete block wall, the lime and earthen plaster of the walls, and the sand-set brick pavers. The heat is retained within the space by the insulated glass and the strawbales that surround the space.

The timber frame teaching pavilion to the north of the building is covered with corrugated polycarbonate, and the trellis-like timber roof gives the gardens an open-air pavilion to teach youth about organic gardening. When it is hot, people can come in from the gardens and sit under shade for respite.

Lime plaster was chosen for the finish material due to its durability and compatibility with the earthen-plaster substrate. It also shares vapor transpirability, similar to the earthen plaster, and will serve to keep the bales dry and mold free.

The timber frame trellis of the pavilion supports a clear polycarbonate roof and provides shade for gardeners during hot summer days.

Finished teaching pavilion as it appeared two hours after the timber frame raising began.

Timber frame detail showing post and knee braces with pegs that secure the mortise-and-tenon joints.

A two-hour timber frame–raising party concluded the construction of greenhouse and learning center.

The first coat of earthen plaster covering the exterior of the greenhouse. The posts and beams, which support the roof, are still seen, as well as the bamboo pinning, which is tied to both sides of the strawbales.

An overall view from the south, with the original classroom wing to the west and the community hall to the east.

School on the Roaring Fork

Waldorf School • Carbondale, Colorado

Our Story

"Waldorf's goal is to kindle a student's passion for discovery that will last a lifetime, and we wanted a building to reflect that philosophy. We acquired thirteen acres four miles east of Carbondale, Colorado, in 1996.

"There we built four buildings incrementally on this site over a period of eight years. The 5,744-square-foot classroom building was first built in 1997 in four and a half months by volunteers and contractors. A labor of love, the largest strawbale building in the United States was constructed on time and within budget.

"During the summer of 2000, we built an early childhood center. In 2001, we began a community hall that we added to the classroom wing for performances, festivals, and other community celebrations. The most recent addition was another classroom building to the east.

"We strove for and achieved a very energy-efficient, passively heated, and lighted set of buildings that minimized the use of wood. We used nontoxic materials in the remainder of the facility. Our school's interior is an interaction between form, light, and color. None of the classrooms are square, but are angled to help the children focus. Natural lighting comes in through windows and skylights.

"Warm colors were used for the lower grades to encourage young children who still live in a fully open, pictorial consciousness. The classrooms for older children, who have begun to think in abstract terms, feature cool colors created with organic casein paints and natural pigment washes. The building's ambiance has contributed greatly to our educational process."

—Waldorf School

Circulation hallways are bright, warm, and friendly.

Specifications	
Exterior Area:	20,000 Total Square Feet in Four Structures
Interior Area:	17,000 +/-
Designer / Architect:	Jeff Dickinson
Contractor / Builder	Waldorf School with Project Managers for Each Phase
Structural System:	Post and Beam
Exterior Plaster:	Cement Stucco
Interior Plaster:	Gypsum
Bales:	Wheat Straw Laid Flat

175

Multibuilding Strawbale Campus

At Waldorf, the strawbale buildings reflect and promote educational values. There are no dark, straight halls filled with lockers and fluorescent lights here. Waldorf School's design was inspired by anthrosophic architecture that fosters spirituality and healing. This inspiration can be felt as the classrooms, halls, and buildings interact with their natural surroundings and welcome you. The classroom wings are designed to allow natural light deep into each non-rectangular, uniquely colored space. Each classroom leads directly outdoors, allowing students to interact with nature daily.

The buildings look more residential than institutional with their low, sloping roofs, generous overhangs, and spread-out plan. A muted sandstone-colored exterior plaster also supports the overall ambiance.

You can feel the open, explorative atmosphere while observing the students' enthusiasm and energy.

The early childhood center was the second building constructed. It is smaller in scale than the other buildings in the complex. The edges of the roof are brought close to the ground and reflect a smaller residential scale for the younger children.

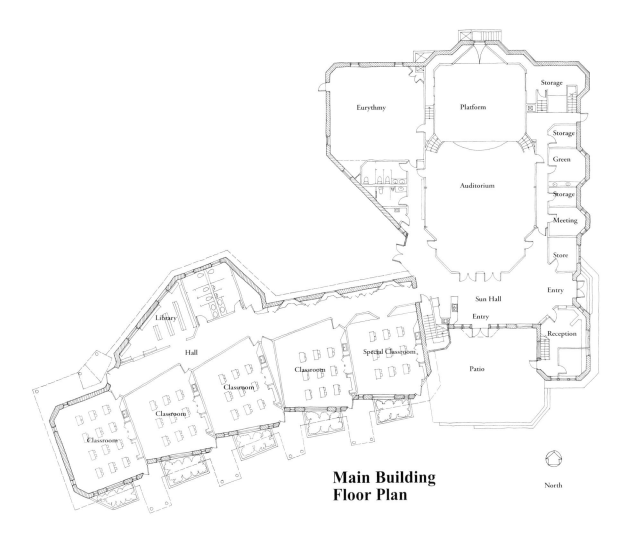

**Main Building
Floor Plan**

Eurythmy

Platform

Storage

Storage

Green

Storage

Meeting

Auditorium

Store

Entry

Sun Hall

Entry

Reception

Library

Special Classroom

Hall

Patio

Classroom

Classroom

Classroom

Classroom

North

The separate classroom building, which provided additional space as the school grew, was the fourth phase to be built.

Classrooms up to fourth grade are painted in the warm spectrum to encourage the young students, who still live in a fully open, pictorial consciousness.

Classrooms for grades five to eight are painted in cooler hues. Students in these grades have begun to think and act in more abstract terms.

Community Buildings

The hand-carved entry doors tell of the unique character of the
natural building and the educational institution within.

Resources

Architects and Designers

Ken Anderson
Edge Environmental Design Group
Enterprise
PO Box 2483
Taos, NM 87571
505.758.5642
www.edgearchitects.com

Wayne J. Bingham, Architect
1444 Michigan Ave.
Salt Lake City, UT 84105
801.583.1370
801.557.4212
wjbingham.com
wjbingham@comcast.net

Kari K. Bremer
Natural & Green Design
PO Box 3753
Durango, CO 81302
970.382.8555
www.naturalgreendesign.com
info@naturalgreendesign.com

Jeff Dickinson
Energy and Sustainable Design
0505 Crystal Circle
Carbondale, CO 81623
970.963.0114

Mark Giorgetti
Palo Santo Designs
108 1/2 Huddleson St.
Santa Fe, NM 87501
505.989.5776 (Santa Fe)
505.737.2824 (Taos)
www.palosantodesigns.com

Doug Graybeal AIA
Graybeal Architects LLC
0188 Sunset Ln.
Carbondale, CO 81623
970.704.1188
www.graybealarchitects.com

Meghan Hanson
PO Box 669
Victor, ID 83455
307.690.6618
meghan@hansonrendering.com

Susie Harrington and Kalen Jones
GAIA Design
PO Box 264
Moab, UT 84532
435.259.7073
www.withgaia.com

Michael Hassig
A4 Architects LLC
242 N. Seventh St.
Carbondale, CO 81623
970.963.6760

Trey Jordan
Conway Jordan Design
161 S. Armijo Ln.
Santa Fe, NM 87501
505.983.5624
www.treyjordan.com

Paula Baker Laporte
PO Box 864
Tesuque, NM 87574
505.984.2928
www.econest.com

Kenton Peters II
KP2 Architects
232 South Dubel Ct.
Salt Lake City, UT 84111
801.359.4048

Dave Powell
Timberline Engineering
PO Box 631
Carbondale, CO 81623
970.963.9869

Donna L. Riley, Architect
PO Box 2066
Carbondale, CO 81623
970.963.7207

Carl Schreiner
19818 Van Dorn
Eagle, NE 68347
402.781.2491

Christopher Stafford
Christopher Stafford Architects
1044 Water St. #326
Port Townsend, WA 98368
360. 379.8541
www.buildinggreen.net

Other Resources

International Straw Bale Registry
http://sbregistry.greenbuilder.com

The Last Straw Journal and Annual
Resource Guide
PO Box 22706
Lincoln, NE 68542
402.483.5135
www.thelaststraw.org

Solar Energy International
PO Box 715
Carbondale, CO 81623
970.964.8866
www.solarenergy.org

Printed Materials

Baker-Laporte, Paula, and Robert Laporte.
*Econest: Creating Sustainable Sanctuaries
of Clay, Straw, and Timber*. Salt Lake City,
UT: Gibbs Smith, Publisher, 2005.

Eisenberg, David. *Straw Bale Construction
and the Building Codes*. 1995.

Book can be ordered from:
Development Center for Appropriate
Technology
PO Box 27513
Tucson, AZ 85726
520.624.6628
www.dcat.net

Ecological Building Network
Collection of over forty papers from the
International Conference on Ecological
Building Structure on CD-Rom.
www.ecobuildnetwork.org

King, Bruce. *Buildings of Earth and Straw*.
Sausalito, CA: Ecological Design Press,
1997.

MacDonald, S. O., and Matts Myhrman.
Build It with Bales. Version Two. White
River Junction, VT: Chelsea Green
Publishing Company, 1997.

Roberts, Carolyn. *A House of Straw: A
Natural Building Odyssey*. White River
Junction, VT: Chelsea Green Publishing
Company, 2002.

Roy, Rob. *Mortgage Free: Radical
Strategies for Home Ownership*. White
River Junction, VT: Chelsea Green
Publishing Company, 1998.

Steen, Bill, and Athena Swentzell Steen.
The Beauty of Straw Bale Homes. White
River Junction, VT: Chelsea Green
Publishing Company, 2000.

Steen, Bill, Athena Swentzell Steen, and
Wayne J. Bingham. *Small Strawbale:
Natural Homes, Projects & Designs*. Salt
Lake City, UT: Gibbs Smith, Publisher,
2005.

Steen, Bill, Athena Swentzell Steen, David
Bainbridge, and David Eisenberg. *The
Straw Bale House*. White River Junction,
VT: Chelsea Green Publishing Company,
1994.

Wanek, Catherine. *The New Strawbale
Home*. Salt Lake City, UT: Gibbs Smith,
Publisher, 2003.

Web Sites

The Canelo Project
HC1 Box 324
Elgin, AZ 85611
520.455.5548
www.caneloproject.com

Colorado Straw Bale
Association/COSBA
2010 Hermosa Dr.
Boulder, CO 80304
303.444.6027
www.coloradostrawbale.org

Fox Maple School of Traditional
Building
PO Box 249
Brownfield, ME 04010
207.935.3720
www.foxmaple.com

International Institute for Bau-Biologie
and Ecology
1401 A Cleveland St.
Clearwater, FL 33755
727.461.4371
www.bau-biologieusa.com

Photo Credits

Audubon Center, 160 (bottom)
Carruthers, Charlie, 114
Fioretti, Susanna, 140 (top), 141 (top and bottom left)
Garrett, Scott and Victoria, 149
Harrrington, Susie, and Kalen Jones, 100 (top)
McClure, Marjorie, 169
O'Brien, Mary and Bob, 37
Petersen, Stan and Jana, 110 (right)
Pruitt, Michael, and Sandra Stowell, 121
Sudmeier, Pat, front cover, 50 (all)
Todd Pierce Photography, 64, 66, 67, 69 (right), 70, 71